# Jonny Wilkinson

# HOW TO PLAY RUGBY

## MY WAY

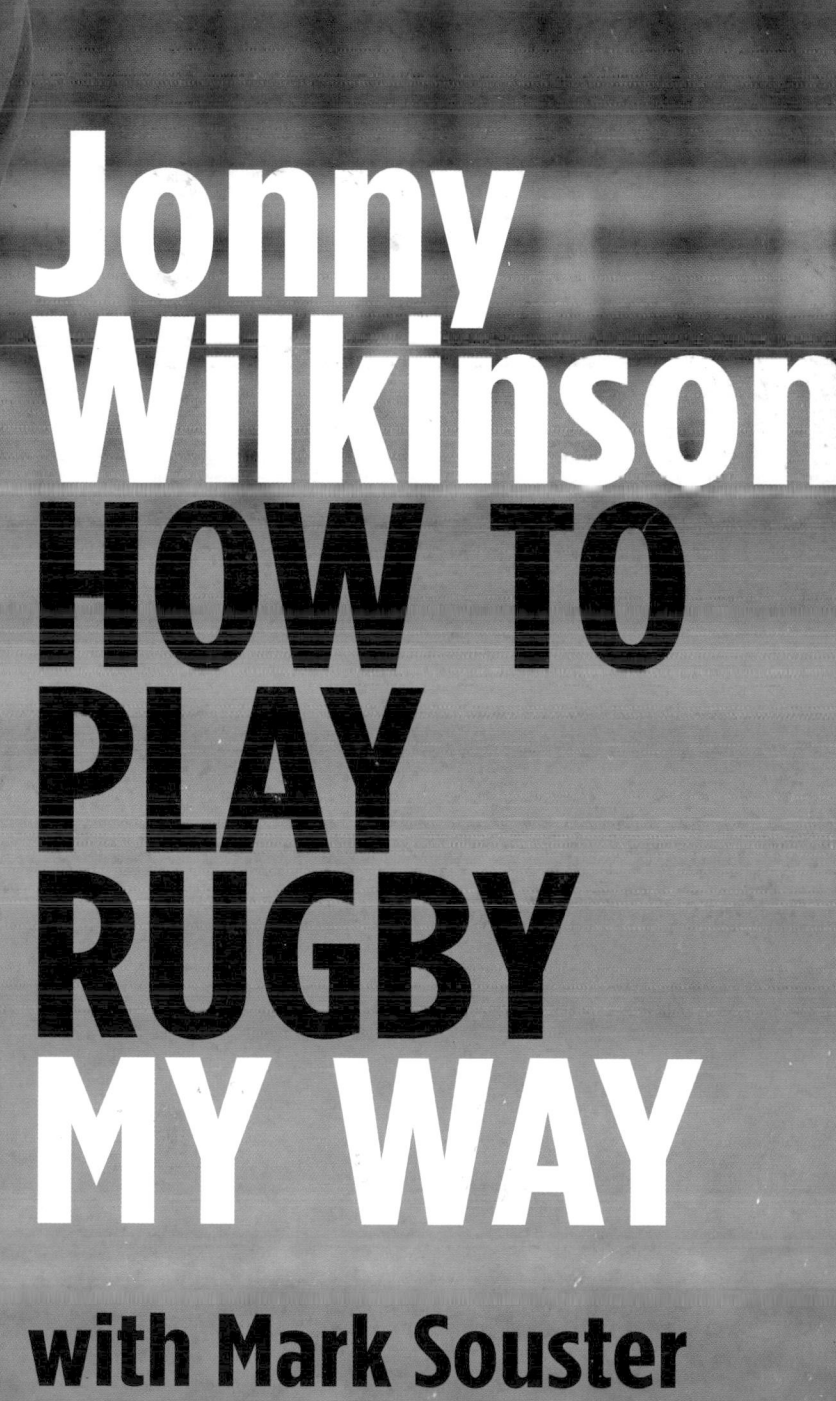

# Jonny Wilkinson
# HOW TO PLAY RUGBY MY WAY

## with Mark Souster

headline

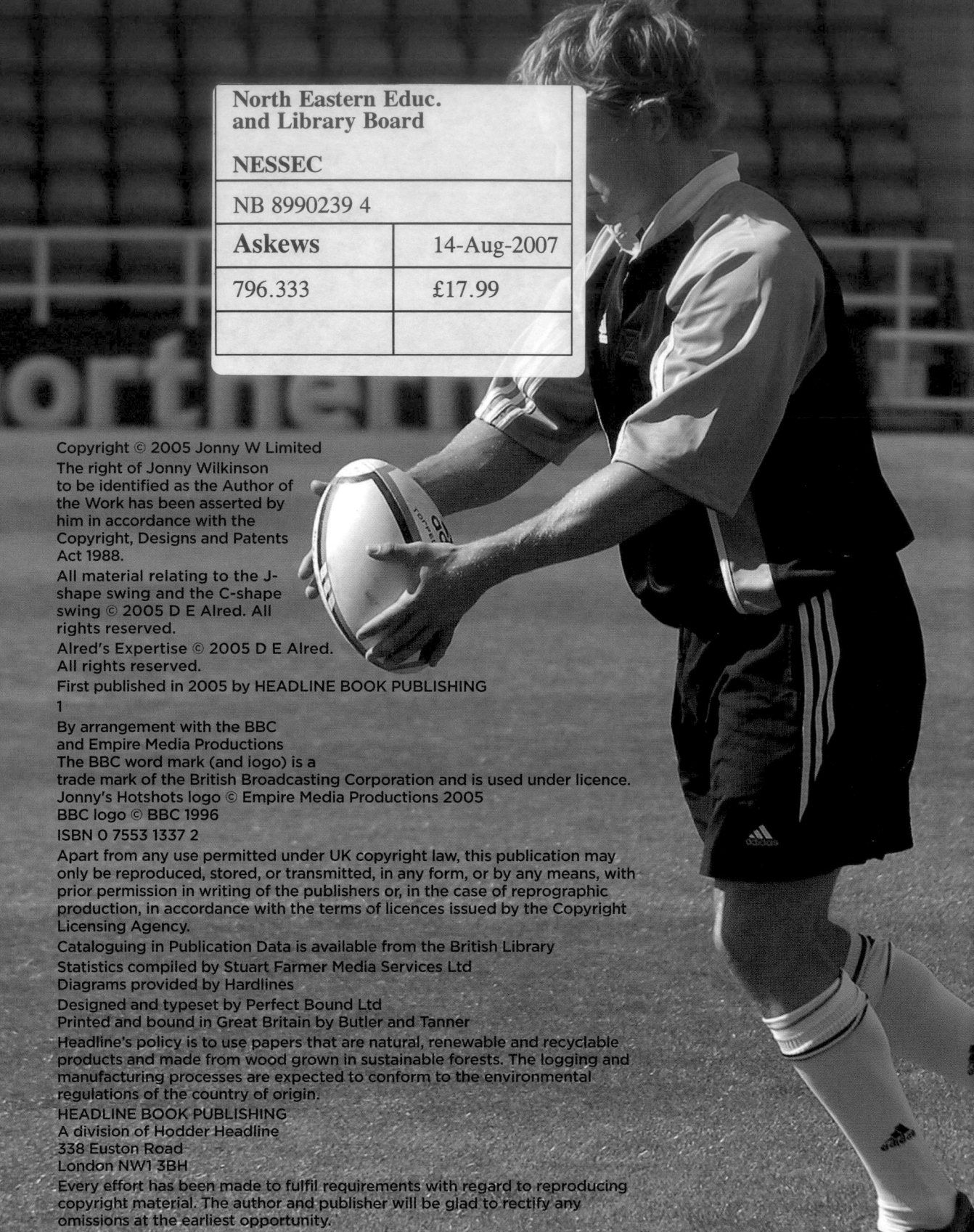

First published in 2005 by HEADLINE BOOK PUBLISHING

1

By arrangement with the BBC
and Empire Media Productions
The BBC word mark (and logo) is a
trade mark of the British Broadcasting Corporation and is used under licence.
Jonny's Hotshots logo © Empire Media Productions 2005
BBC logo © BBC 1996

ISBN 0 7553 1337 2

Statistics compiled by Stuart Farmer Media Services Ltd
Diagrams provided by Hardlines

Designed and typeset by Perfect Bound Ltd
Printed and bound in Great Britain by Butler and Tanner

Headline's policy is to use papers that are natural, renewable and recyclable
products and made from wood grown in sustainable forests. The logging and
manufacturing processes are expected to conform to the environmental
regulations of the country of origin.

HEADLINE BOOK PUBLISHING
A division of Hodder Headline
338 Euston Road
London NW1 3BH

www.headline.co.uk
www.hodderheadline.com

# Contents

# Introduction

This book is not just for budding Hotshots. It's for anyone interested in rugby and is intended to work on a number of levels. If you've just taken up the game, you can use it to get a grip on the basics and start to develop your skills. If you are young but have been playing for a while there's loads here that might sound generally familiar, but I think you will find that the ideas and techniques go deeper than you might be used to and you can use those aspects to take your game on further. And if you are at a more advanced level of play already you will definitely find elements here which you can absorb, take out what you need and adapt them to the level you are playing at.

For those of you who are learning the skills at 8–12 years old, the principles are exactly the same as for those playing the game aged 15, 25 or even 30. The only difference is that the older players will be stronger. But just because someone aged 20 can kick further than someone aged 10, the techniques outlined in the book still apply as both players will always need accuracy in the kick. Kicking a long way in the wrong direction isn't much good to anyone. The fundamental principles of how to play the game successfully are the same regardless of age – and they are always worth learning and relearning.

The great thing, I think, is that as players begin to understand the game and the skills, and improve their game play, they'll be able to take more and more out of the book. They'll relate more and more to the points made here and develop them on their own. And for those who have greater mastery of the basics, there are also expert tips for things to work on.

## Why I wrote the book

I want to pass on my experiences and the knowledge I've learned and been taught. It is that simple. I'm also interested in introducing a new way of thinking about the skills I am going to be talking about. When I've reached for rugby textbooks in the past, or have gone on coaching courses, they've been great – but they have been fairly similar. I think that I view the game from a different angle, perhaps because I have learned so much from playing against so many great teams, and also from the fact that in my career I've enjoyed the highest of highs and endured the lowest of lows – I've learned from losing as much as I have from winning.

And of course I have been incredibly lucky to have been guided in my game by Steve Black (my training coach, who most of the time I call Blackie) and Dave Alred (my kicking coach). They will crop up a fair bit throughout the book. And on top of all that, there is all the stuff I've worked on with my brother Mark

(he'll be referred to as Sparks from now on). I hope there is something in that combination that will help me get the message over.

I also love the idea of coaching and passing on ideas. If I can help anyone with this book, that will be a great achievement for me. This is especially true of the kicking chapters, as I know what it's like to be a kicker and to be confused as to why you are not striking the ball well or missing the target, or why you are hitting one out of three instead of three out of three. I've been playing the game and practising for so long that it just seems a waste not to try and pass on all that knowledge and experience, especially to youngsters who can have a lot longer than I had to try and develop their game and see what they want to do with it.

I guess it all boils down to hoping to be able to help the game that's helped me. I want to make sure that I don't miss any opportunity to use the entire potential of this Hotshots project to reach players of any age and offer them the chance to learn a bit and certainly enjoy the game more. I am also keen on improving the general understanding of the game to a wider world and, by raising awareness, I am hoping that rugby's following will also increase. Getting more and more parents into the game so that they can coach and really support their kids would certainly be a huge achievement and benefit for the sport. And through all of this, ideally what will happen is that we get into a cycle – the more interest in the game, the bigger the game gets, and the bigger it gets, the more interest is generated. That's what I want to accomplish above all.

Blackie, about to put Matt Baker from Blue Peter through his paces

HOW TO PLAY RUGBY MY WAY

## Cover to cover?

This is not a book that has to be read cover-to-cover in a week. I hope you'd enjoy doing that, for sure, but more to the point, I see it as a book that you can dip in and out of, looking at different aspects. That way you can spend time on one thing and focus on that chapter until you think that you've made some progress. Then you can move on to something new. I'd love the book to inspire people to think, 'I want to go do a session down at the local pitch and I want to work on my agility, so I want to have a look at some of those drills'; or, 'Me and my mates want to do a bit of passing, we'll go and concentrate on that'; or go kicking and say, 'I've had a bit of a problem with my kicking today. I just want to check again what I should work on tomorrow.'

That's what I do in my head, to be honest. I'll do a skill, say kicking, and if certain things aren't going right, I'll correct them, so that by the end of the session things will be going better. Then when I start the next session, the first thing in my head is, 'What must I think about before I start?' It's pointless for me to go firing into another kicking session, and think halfway through, 'Oh, at the end of yesterday, I was really concentrating on this aspect.' So it's important that at the start of each session you concentrate on what you were working on at the end of the previous session and consolidating on that to improve.

## What to get out of the book

I'm not a specialist, I'd never presume that. All I am saying with this book is that this is what I've learned from playing against New Zealand and Australia, from playing in World Cups and Lions tours. These are the things I've picked up from a lifetime with people like Dave Alred

and Martin Johnson, and understanding the way they think about things. All the different points I bring up in the book have come about through winning Grand Slams, from losing Grand Slams, from winning World Cups, from losing World Cups. Some of it is information that people have given to me and I've processed it and turned it into how I've wanted to use it. Other parts are information that I've created myself, things I've sat and thought about and I'm offering it to other people and saying, 'Do with it what you will.' Take the ideas that work for you and maybe add your own bits. In a nutshell, this book is all about the things that have worked for me and I hope that at least some aspects of them will work equally well for you.

Perhaps someone will take this information and they'll think, 'Oh yeah, that's really helpful but I'd quite like to do this.' That's fine. Or even if people read some of the material and think, 'I probably wouldn't do it that way, but now I can see what I should do instead.' Adapt the techniques to suit you, that's the secret.

I learned some of the ideas in this book when I was 16 or 17, and I've worked on them since. But if people can get this book aged 10 or 11, by the time they get to 16 or 17, it will be natural behaviour for them. My problem was that by the time I became a teenager I thought I'd learned some of the skills because I'd been practising them for so long. But when I met people like Dave, who wanted to teach me a better way of doing things, I realised I had to relearn a great deal. I had to go backwards in order to come forwards. That's fine, and it is certainly achievable. Older players shouldn't be put off by that reassessment process. For younger players, what I hope with this book is that they have the opportunity to process all the collected knowledge that's here before they get into bad habits.

Sparks probably laughing at one of his own jokes

That is me on the right playing full back for Farnham on a very small pitch!

In the grand scheme of things it will be very interesting to see how this learning affects younger players who will be coming through in future years. They could be people working on various skills now, evolving them and adapting them to their special style. I'd like to think in a few years some of those individuals – who have been practising passing, kicking, tackling, running attacking lines – will become multi-skilled and creative players. If that happens, by the time they emerge in the professional ranks they'll be able to take the skills to the next level, whatever that is, and the game will reach new heights.

Acquiring and developing rugby skills can be a bit like assembling a jigsaw, which occasionally gets knocked out of place. One or two pieces come loose and you have to open up

the box – which is the process of training – search for which pieces have become unstuck and work on getting them back in place. For example, with kicking you might become unhappy with where your chest finishes, how the ball felt off your foot, what it looked like in flight, what sort of noise did it make, etc. When you've found the piece that is missing you can push it back in and feel confident that by the time you get to the game your jigsaw is complete again. And that's the way to look at this book. Let it help you find and sort out that one piece which has slipped out of place, until it becomes second nature.

## Trust yourself

I think that playing rugby comes in two parts. There's the side of the rugby player that does his preparation, all the hard work off the field. And then there's the side of the rugby player that goes on the field and performs under pressure and reacts to what happens. The player that does all the preparation is a bit more like a businessman. That's your preparation, building your power as a player, except with rugby it's actually good fun, which makes a change. The player that goes onto the field for kickoff is your natural talent. This part of you now has the ability to use the extra power created by the business side of practice and preparation.

There are only so many things you can work on for a game. You can't cover every base because you never know what's round the corner. That's actually one of the best things about rugby. You never know what'll happen next. But you can prepare as best you can so that when something does happen, you react to it.

You've got to trust yourself and you've got to reward yourself. When you do something well in a game, don't just think, 'Well, I should have done that well because I've practised.' You need to practise, sure, but having done so it takes loads of talent to go out there and react under pressure. What you should never do is lose faith or trust in that individual natural ability. Don't let training and preparation take away from the trust.

This is a mistake that I fell into. I started to feel that if I didn't have time or wasn't able to do my 120 punts or 500 goal kicks then I'd never be able to kick a ball in a game. What you've got to understand is training does matter, which is why you've got to do it, why you need to do it, and it does improve you and does give you a better chance of doing well. But you've also got to sit down and realise the kicks you get in games are because you've got a talent, and that talent takes over when the whistle goes. The businessman only helps it. He doesn't make it. Practice doesn't make a player, it only helps a player. That for me is the key.

Always trust yourself, your natural ability, and be confident and go out there and express yourself. Don't step on to the pitch fearing failure and don't try and have too many superstitions. There is no substitute for trusting your own ability. Some people might think that if they don't put their left sock on first then they won't kick well, that sort of thing. It's rubbish. Because if that's what makes a great player, putting your left sock on first, there would be 2 or 3 million fantastic rugby players out there.

But most importantly, go out and enjoy the game. I fell in love with rugby many years ago – I hope this book takes you some way to doing the same.

# Practice
## and training

# Practice and training

I t might seem odd to outline my ideas on practice and training before we've even begun to look at what the key skills are in playing rugby, but I think it is important, right at the outset, to have in the back of your mind how you might go about learning and refining the techniques outlined later in the book. This should allow you to envisage how you could go about setting up training drills, practice sessions and a fitness programme that will suit you.

And that is the point here. This chapter deals with my views on practice and training – well, mine and Blackie's to be more accurate. Everyone is different: age, ability, access to resources, time available. I am not suggesting that this is how everyone should develop their rugby skills. You have to sort out your own methods, depending on all the various factors that relate to you.

So I haven't set out specific routines or exercises. What I have done is explain how I try to be the best I can and I have tried to explain the key points that I feel are important. This is how I play rugby my way. How you approach it will be up to you. But I hope this helps you focus on what you want to achieve.

## Why practise?

The most important thing is to practise well. It is quality rather than quantity. It's not the number of things you do or even the time you're there. Practice is all about getting as good as you can be, as quickly as you can.

HOW TO PLAY RUGBY MY WAY

Before any player can practise safely and effectively it is vital time is taken to prepare the body for the work that he intends to do. This is called warming up and while there is definitely no set routine for a warmup there are some very important guidelines to follow.

First of all, it is important to get the body warm. This is why it is key to start by jogging. Some teams keep exercise bikes on the sidelines as alternative means of keeping warm. So begin slowly and gradually pick up a little more pace – continue to feel yourself breathing a little more heavily and feel the blood circulating around the muscles in your legs and arms. Once warm it is then imperative you initiate the type of movements you will be using in your session but begin gently and slowly, again gradually building up the intensity. For example, if you plan to kick then begin with running with high knees, heel flicks and side to side movements. Then some small leg swings and later some higher leg swings. For an agility session – high knees, heel flicks and then some gentle changes of direction building up to include spins and large lateral movements. For tackling – think about preparing the upper body as well by beginning with swinging your arms in all directions, gently push against an opponent and build to include press ups. Another idea here would be to practise dropping to the floor and quickly getting back up again, thus preparing your body for contact and collisions.

Take time to warm up and do it thoroughly. As I will mention later in the book, there is very little you can do about injuries that come about through contact but you can prevent muscle tears and strains by warming up professionally Missing 6 or 8 weeks of rugby because you did not jog for long enough one morning is not going to be a great feeling.

# Blackie's secrets

Jonny's regime has evolved specifically for him. Initially, we started off with a very general base. We built up the basic strength, muscular endurance and speed. Then we started to look at how he wanted to play the game. We studied different methods of movement and different ways to get stronger in a specific way, so that everything was geared towards him. This means that the training regime that Jonny has isn't off the shelf or out of a book. It's specific and unique to him, which allows it to cover a wider base.

It's about being able to reproduce a skill when you are under pressure, as second nature. You need to create a good foundation of all the basics, then build on them, refine them and fine-tune them. Then it is vital to put yourself under pressure and create realistic game-like situations. If you don't have those basic building blocks in place, you're always going to struggle.

I always think that at the end of the session, however, you need to be feeling pretty good about yourself. This is where an element of self-coaching comes in. For instance, it's not necessarily a good idea to go to kicking practice, kick ten over, then miss five, then kick three over that didn't really feel very good and think, 'Oh, that'll do.' It's more effective to be able to go out there and kick until you feel as if you have total control over where the ball is going and how it is feeling off your foot, then

leave. Only you will know when that moment is. That might be 40 minutes. For me it tends to be a bit longer! But then again, I have more time than most – this is my job after all.

If things aren't going well in, say, your passing, and you have thrown ten in a row that just didn't feel right, you need to be aware of this and not just ignore the fact and keep on at it or decide you are done. You need to be thinking 'Right, hold on, I need to go back and throw ten more and really concentrate this time on some key points. And then later today, I'm going to throw another ten, to make

sure I've really got it.' Blackie has this analogy about business. A lot of businesses just churn out the same old plans and performance memos to their staff despite the fact that when they are asked about them they admit that they are not really used or referred to. So what is the point? It is wasted energy. Just like carrying on the passing routines when deep down you know there is a problem. It might seem like the correct thing to do, to put the repetitions in, but it is not working. Taking a break to focus on the key basics and putting them right, that is good use of time and resources.

## Blackie's secrets

In rugby you need to be strong, powerful, quick and have fast reactions, coordination, agility and balance. Your conditioning needs to reflect all of this. Lots of people do lots of training, they become compulsive at it, going through endless fitness tests, for example. These athletes train to get better for the fitness tests, rather than for the activity they're training for. We don't do any fitness tests. We tailor our session to the way Jonny is feeling. We've got such a good relationship that if he's feeling great, he tells me. If he's not, he'll tell me that as well, and we adapt accordingly. But everything is always transferable to the pitch.

# The mental toughness, as well as the physical exertion of training, is very important.

### Why train?

Well, apart from the need to build strength and stamina, I think a major point of training is being able to strengthen yourself mentally – to be able to push yourself outside your comfort zones. What I'm talking about is being able to understand what it feels like to think you can't go on, but then actually to manage to do so, to go further; or to be able to approach a session knowing that it's going to be incredibly tough and that you're going to be in some sort of stress or discomfort, yet, not to fear that session, to actually look forward to it. That sort of attitude training, mental toughness if you like, can be the difference between winning and losing. What you want to develop is the kind of mindset that says, in the last five minutes of a game when the score is tied, 'Give me the ball' rather than 'I wish this was all over, I can't do any more.' Winners and losers are made right there. So the mental toughness, as well as the physical exertion of training, is very important.

### My attitude to practising and training

As I said earlier, I think it is important to make sure you leave the practice session with a feeling that you are in control of whatever skill it is that you have been working on. That said, you also need to be able to listen to your body and change your practising if it's necessary.

Suppose you wake up in the morning thinking, 'I'm going to go kicking today. I'm really going to do a good session,' but when you get to the park, it's pouring down, it's freezing, and you hear yourself say, 'I don't want to do

it.' That's the point where you need to assess what's making you say that. Is it because your body doesn't feel right? Fine, then you can adjust your original plans so you can still train, but do it in a different location or maybe a session with less impact. It is also fine to just take the day off. Mind you, if I am honest, I'm not very good at taking breaks, but it's important to recognise when you need one. I find it difficult to sit at home and think, 'I could be out there,' especially when it's a beautiful day. It kills me, but sometimes you just know you're

not right. It's the importance of understanding what your body is telling you.

But if you're thinking you'll give it a miss because the weather has changed and for no other reason, I think that's again where mental toughness comes into play.

If instead of thinking, 'I just don't fancy this,' you can say, 'OK, the weather's changed and it won't be as pleasant, but I'll go out there and do it,' that's when some of those ses-

## Blackie's secrets

In rugby there's lots of physical confrontation, and where there's confrontation and conflict, emotions can spill over. Jonny's never do, which is absolutely fantastic. It isn't spoken about a lot, but he's always got that in check, because he knows that's the best way to operate in that environment. He's not a cold, heartless, emotionless person himself, quite the contrary. But he's able to have great discipline within the competitive arena, meaning that he can utilise everything that happens in that environment optimally, to produce a performance that will allow victory. He's very much into effectiveness.

sions become the most beneficial. You know that other people will be sitting inside the clubhouse or at home, asking, 'How on earth does he do that?' And yet you're out there. They're saying, 'Oh, I'd hate to be him right now,' and you're actually thinking, 'This is brilliant,' because you're taking on the elements and really being challenged. That's how I like to feel, as if I'm coming through the challenge. In the same way as when you push yourself in training, that experience of practising when others aren't up for it can be

# You say 'OK, the weather's changed and it won't be as pleasant, but I'll go out there and do it.'

what you draw upon in a game, when you've got the crowd booing and you need a big kick to take the lead. The fact that you've put yourself through every condition whereas your opponent might have skipped their practice because they didn't want to get wet, can really make a difference to your mindset, and ultimately, the outcome of a game.

My attitude to training is pretty much the same. I always want to go the extra mile, and I enjoy it. It's a huge part of my life. It feels right to finish a hard session and to be bent over double, gasping for breath, but at the same time knowing how good you are going to feel about yourself and your ability in 10 minutes' time.

## My routine

When I finish a session, the key for me is to know I've done everything I needed to make me feel like my best at that point in time. By the time I get home I like to have earned my time with my feet up, watching a movie.

# My attitude to training is pretty much the same. I always want to go the extra mile, and I enjoy it.

In a typical day there are several sessions to fit in. I like to train with Blackie, and I'll do that every day, unless we both decide that I need a day off. I also do a team session, rehab on my neck and on my knee, and kicking plus other skills. I quite like to practise skills after the rugby session, because it means there are no guidelines, there is no time limit on me. If I'm having a session where I'm thinking, 'I need to do more of this', or I've kicked indoors for an hour so now I need to go outdoors and finish off in the wind, I can do it without worrying about the time.

Training days run from probably about 9 a.m. to 5 or 6 p.m. They start with rehab or a one or one session with Blackie for 45 minutes or so, then a team meeting at 10 a.m., team training from 10.30 a.m. until 11.30 a.m. This is followed by lunch until 1 p.m. and after that I will do kicking for an hour and then at 2 p.m. it's a team rugby session until 4 p.m. Then to finish I do kicking and personal skills until 5 or 6 p.m.

# I may focus on a specific aspect to make sure I have it spot on.

But just to reiterate, I'm not suggesting everyone should, or can, follow this schedule. It works for me because rugby is my profession. Most people will only have opportunities in the evenings or at weekends – you just need to fit in your routine when you can. A different session each day may be the answer. If you are busy, a 20-minute passing session would be a great idea, and is still very fulfilling as long as it is done with intense focus on precision.

## Kicking practice

In my role within the team, this is obviously one of the key skills for me and I spend a lot of time on my technique. There are different ways that I work on improving my kicking. I work by myself, and with other people. One of those is my kicking coach, Dave Alred, who helps me out a great deal. I speak to him about once a week, letting him know how I feel my kicks have been going and receiving feedback and suggestions on how I can improve and iron out any problems I've noticed.

I like to do a bit of kicking with people as it is more fun and you don't have to go off and retrieve all those balls! Just collecting, say, 20 balls from the stands if I have been practising drop goals on my own cuts significantly into the time available to practise.

Dave Alred keeping a watchful eye over one of my kicking sessions. I wonder what he'd give me out of ten for that one?

Mind you, one thing I find difficult about kicking with other people is that there's not a lot of opportunity to kick off both feet equally, which is important in game play. For example, if I am kicking to the left-hand touch line with my left foot, and the balls are being picked up and kicked back by a team mate then I get less chance to go down to that touch line and practise kicking back up with my right foot. If I am on my own, I'd be doing that, hitting touchline, touchline, touchline, touchline, and kicking with both feet. It is also asking a lot from a one-footed kicker to kick for as long as it takes for

me to be happy with both my feet.

It's important to keep variety in the session and I think there's a huge amount to be said for combining game realism. For example, we do a good practice where I'll kick to the touchline, then I'll kick one drop punt, one running drop punt, one spiral, one running spiral and then start again. So you never kick two the same. I sometimes vary this a bit by placing 20 or so balls around the pitch, moving to each one to execute a different kick under pressure from a team mate. That way

you never get into that golf driving range mentality where it's all just smash, smash, smash, smash, smash, because in rugby you don't get that luxury.

If there's a game coming up, I may focus on a specific aspect to make sure I have it spot on. For instance, if there's a chance of heavy wind at the weekend, I may feel that I really need to leave knowing that my weight shift through the ball is absolutely fantastic, so I might spend an hour just working on that particular component. At the end of the session

*I know one of my kicks landed up here. I was aiming for this seat. But I can't see it anywhere*

I'll know – hopefully – that I have achieved my goal. That's a great feeling.

## Train to be more effective

I started training at about 12 years old, getting more serious towards about 15 or 16. Then when I came up to Newcastle, I met Blackie, and realised it hadn't been serious at all. I thought I was working at a level 9 out of 10, then I started with Blackie and realised that the scale goes up to 50 or even 100 and I was still working at 9.

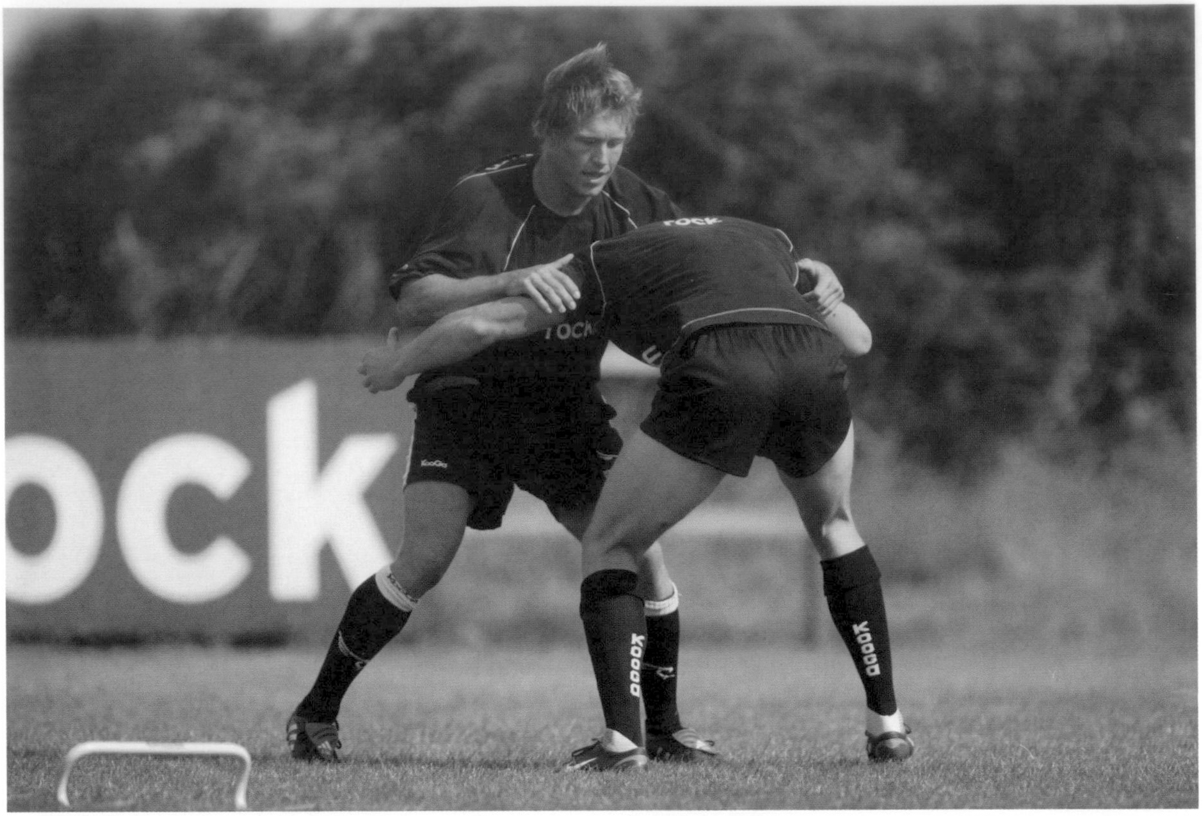

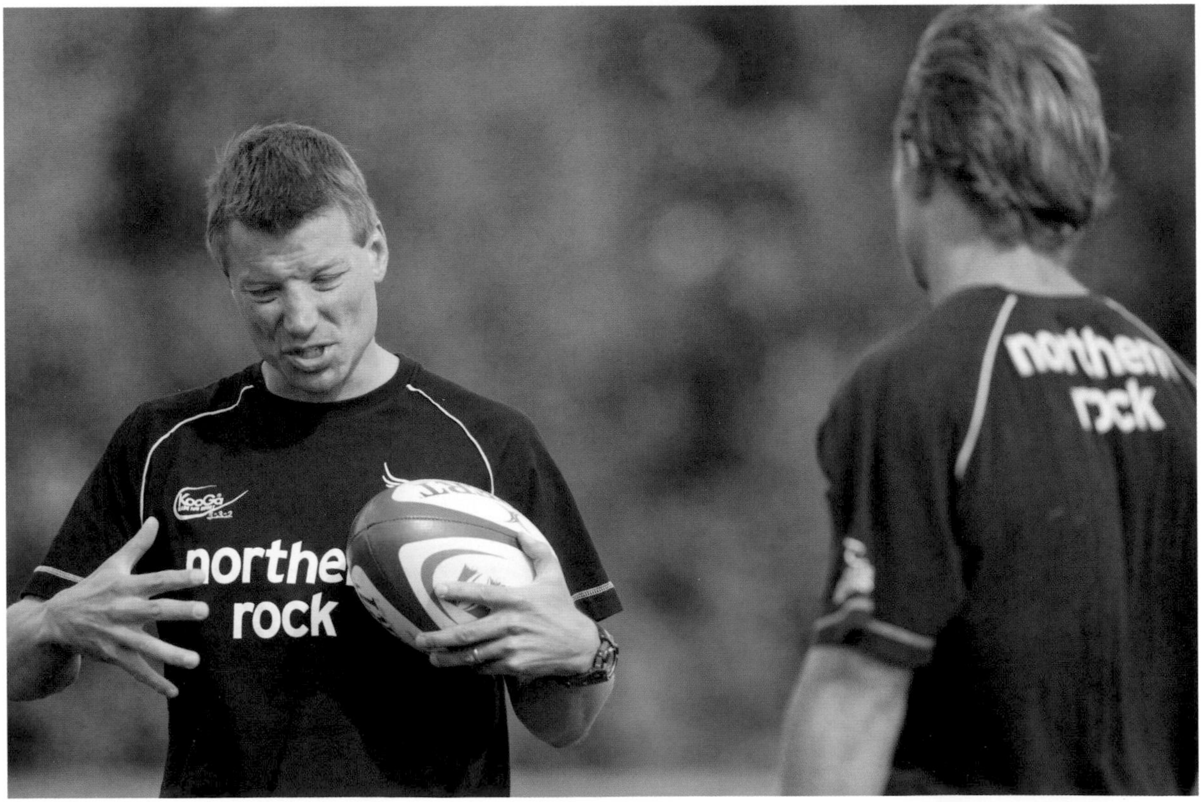
rock

Blackie's always there for me, and for all the guys he trains. I could call him at 2 a.m. – I haven't done that yet – and he'd be there. His dedication and commitment are superb. The amount of respect and admiration I have for Blackie means that there's certainly no way I'm ever going to let him down which means I train so much more intensely. I can be totally destroyed in 5 minutes if he wants, and other times it takes 10 minutes. He knows how to get the very best out of me because of the time he spends with me, and that's the same for any other person he's involved with.

We train in a very game-specific way. Every-thing we do is thought out clearly as to how it could help me out there on the field. Every little exercise has a purpose. We don't train for too long, but we train fast and very intensely, much like a game.

In rugby you need to be able to work very hard in short periods, to be very powerful, and then be very very effective in recovering in the short time you have available to you. So we push hard, and then often when I'm at my most tired, he'll get me to perform a fairly dif-ficult skill. By doing that, he helps me to toughen up mentally, and to understand that I need to be able to perform under serious pressure, and serious fatigue.

Blackie's sessions aim at getting you to perform at the most difficult times in a game. There's lots of passing under pressure – being harried by defenders, quick hands etc. – but we also concentrate on being able to catch and pass when you are at your most tired. This is where the basic technical aspects of the skill, that I will be detailing later in the book, become critical. Just because you're tired doesn't mean that a pass can loop or land too high. You have to master the core skill and if it becomes second nature, no matter how exhausted you are in a game you can still rely on getting the ball away effectively. You've got to challenge yourself in those situations as well – push yourself and find out where your limits are.

With tackling, we often hone our basic skills on tackle bags but I tend to do a lot of 1-on-1 stuff, working with Sparks or one of the other guys like Matthew Tait or Jamie Noon. It is simple, but very effective. I get one of them to run at me, attempting to get past me, and I try and take him down. Other times the team will work just a yard out from the try line. One person will try to lunge over and we've got to hit them and keep them up. Another important element is to be able to make a tackle and get straight up on your feet again. We do a lot of work on the floor that simulates defensive work – up, no tackle, back off, back onside, down on the floor, up again, go again, then a big long run, weave in and out, stop. That feels just like a game. We also do a lot of stuff with a rugby ball. Passing, stop, run again, catch, pass, run again, catch, pass. It's great because you're focusing on the ball and the skills and don't realise how hard you're working.

## Blackie's secrets

In training, we try to use the Japanese model, Kaizen, which is the idea of continuous improvement. Jonny enjoys what he does enormously and that helps him move towards his potential. We talk about trying to improve day by day because you will never be at your best every day. We understand that people who believe they have already reached their peak are actually mediocre. So, the point is to try and be the best that you can be on any given day, and work towards improving that level.

There's also the need to replicate attacking play. For this, we play a lot of touch games – 3-on-2s, 4-on-3s, 3-on-3s, 4-on-4s, that sort of thing. Just constantly putting yourself in a situation where you've got to think and you've got to react to what someone else does with a ball. Games of 6-on-6 touch are brilliant for that because people get tired and you have to spot who's the most exhausted, then you can attack them. We call this 'Exploiting the Defence' and spotting a 'miss match', which I'll be going into in more detail in the Attacking chapter. It is a very important element of game play.

It is also important to get used to anticipation in the midst of a game and these touch training sessions really help. You have to understand what the next defender will do when put under pressure and what your own team mates will

do. If I'm outside someone, for example David Walder or Jamie Noon, I know the kind of thing they do with the ball, so I know how to adjust my support line accordingly. But if I'm outside my brother, I'll know he'll do something different, so I can change what I do. You only manage that through putting yourself in the situation in training.

Blackie never really lets you know quite how many reps he wants from you especially in the strength and endurance training. He's more akin to just putting you on the machine and saying 'OK' and just letting you go until you feel like you can't go any more and then he'll say, 'Alright now give me some more.' You'd be surprised how many more you can do when you've got him staring down at you. Other times he'll stop you after only a few reps. Things like that are very important. You're never holding back, never pacing yourself, but always giving everything immediately. I think that's the key to a lot of the work Blackie does – being able to give it absolutely everything, rest, and then give it all again.

**HOW TO PLAY RUGBY MY WAY**

## Blackie's secrets

We look at something we call the 24 hour clock. So, if you were to follow Jonny around for 24 hours with a camera, would he be proud of the video evidence of what he's been doing? Would he behave with integrity all of the time? When he meets people, would he be well mannered and helpful in all aspects of whatever he's doing? This is something that's fuelled his life now for a long time. It is very much who Jonny is. Trying to improve, trying to use his talents, trying to create an environment for himself and his colleagues, that will allow all their talents to flourish collectively together.

# Blackie's sessions aim at getting you to perform at the most difficult times in a game.

In terms of specific exercises and training techniques, Blackie tends to bring in his experiences from outside rugby. For example he brings in a lot of his boxing training and we work on special mats, do lots of balancing, and use trampets. The variety is really important, although sometimes you turn up and he gets you going on a session and you think, 'This is absolute hell,' and yet it's still different and you just get on and enjoy it.

Sometimes he'll get me playing tennis against the wall with these special waffle bats. After my injury, when he was building my arm and shoulder back up, I'd be up there against the side of the stands smashing a tennis ball against the wall, 30 yards away. The ball would come back and I'd have to smash it again, so I was working on my shoulder, but as soon as

he shouted 'Go!', I'd catch the ball, drop the bat, and sprint around the second team pitch as fast as I could. After several repetitions of this you can imagine it gets very tiring.

As soon as I got back he'd say, 'Great, pick the racquet up and off you go again,' until he shouted 'Go!' once more. The first time I hared around the field in about 57 seconds, then he said, 'Right the next one, let's see how close you can get to that.' So I'd smash the ball, sprint round the field and it was 53. Literally, that was the session – but break it down and it makes sense. A difficult specific skill that requires huge concentration and precision that is performed under serious fatigue from an exercise like running round the field to a time limit – that really challenges your mental toughness.

**Skills**

# Passing

# Passing

**P**assing skills are very important. The ball moves quicker than the man, which is why the quality of passing is vital. Moving the ball effectively gives you the advantage, as defenders cannot keep pace. It allows you to create space and get to areas of the pitch before the defenders can cover them – and that leads to tries. Now that's the fun bit. The more you develop your passing, and the more accurate your passing is, the more space and opportunities you get from attacking moves with the ball. There are two types of pass: short and long.

A short pass is best utilised when you're attacking close to the defence, really threatening. It's about passing to a team mate who's either running into a gap or aiming to fix a defender who can then catch the ball and equally quickly move it on. Short passing is an essential skill and you need to be very in tune with the needs of your recipient so that they can catch the ball easily and be in a position to run on to the ball hard, sometimes with a late change of angle or deliver a pass themselves at pace.

Remember, how you execute the pass will determine how they receive it and that in turn will determine whether they can move it on, while under pressure from the defence and with little time to spare. It is therefore important that short passes should not be spun harshly because they will travel too quickly over that short distance and the recipient won't have the time or opportunity to adjust their hands to ensure that the ball is taken at the optimal angle. A spun short pass will take

This is how to hold the ball for a short pass

the recipient by surprise and could easily be dropped or taken on the chest which will stop the flow of the move.

Spin passes tend to be used when you want the ball to travel a longer distance, flat but very quickly, so you can cut out a defender, perhaps by passing across the front of one of your own players to a team mate further out in the line who will now have space to attack in, or throwing to a wide man already in space. Spinning the ball makes it go faster but even still, unless the recipient is completely unmarked, you need to be slightly further back from the line of defence than you would be for a short pass. No matter how well you spin your pass out, the ball still takes time to reach the recipient and if the defence is tight on you they will have a fraction longer to react, potentially halting the attack in its tracks.

## Short passing – how to do it

As shown on the previous page, the ball should be held with your hands on either side, about half way along the length, with your fingers spread. For a pass to your right, put your left foot forward, and your left elbow up. This creates a channel under your left arm. Think of that channel – it is important. When you make your pass, it allows your hands and your fingers to push through towards the target, while still allowing you to attack the defender in a straight line because you don't have to twist.

The top end of the ball (i.e. furthest away from you) can be tilted to the floor (i.e. pointing to 6 o'clock) and the ball is passed by moving your spread fingers towards the target. The arms push the ball directly at the receiver, and the fingers should finish exactly facing, or pointing right to the target.

The ball, from its 6 o'clock position, may also be angled up slightly on release to create a rotation, a back-spinning rotation, which helps the ball travel straight and a little further, if the situation on the pitch requires a longer

pass. You can see the ball angled up on release on page 46. You need to practise both techniques as the play in front and around you changes by the second and you will be far more effective if you have both short-pass and slightly longer-pass weapons in your armoury. This is particularly difficult to defend against as both pass executions look exactly the same.

So, there are two main points to be aware of in short passing. One is to push your hands through to the target and two is to finish with your fingers pointing at the recipient. It is important also to remember holding the corresponding elbow high as this makes life particularly difficult for any defenders to make strong tackles with a barrier like this pointing at them.

If practised well, the passer can learn to spin the ball slowly so that it travels faster and straight and arrives at your intended recipient more or less in the vertical position – and that makes it easier to catch, as you can see on the next page. A flat, non-back spinning pass will float and move in the air over any extended distance, making it more difficult to catch. Remember, in these fast phases of play, you have to make things as easy for your team mates as possible. As play is unfolding around you, there is hardly any time to think, so split seconds count. If your team mate receives the ball at the best possible angle – then you keep the move flowing.

Obviously, all you need to do is swap this technique round for passes out to the left: right foot forward and right elbow up, you create a channel between your right forearm and your right side which allows you to move your hands directly to the receiver, but basically everything else stays the same.

# It seems pointless to me to be involved in a sport and not have a desire to be your best at it.

# The placement of the legs is highly important because not only does it make your passing more effective, it also makes your moves harder to defend against.

## Short passing in action

The weight of your pass needs to be sure. You don't want to pass a ball that's too powerful so that your team mate doesn't have time to move his hands round to receive it, but at the same time if it's wobbling feebly around in the air, your team mate is going to be waiting for it to arrive, which will allow the opposition to read the pass and prepare its defence for a man and ball play-stopping tackle. So the pass needs to be firm, quick but manageable so that it's in the hands nice and easily, and the receiver can react to what's going on in front of them.

The placement of the legs is highly important because not only does it make your passing more effective, it also makes your moves harder to defend against. If I am running towards a defender, with the intention of passing to my right, and I put my left foot forward, it means that I have two options. I can either continue running at the defender and then pass the ball, or I can dummy the pass and continue moving forward at pace. My speed or body position isn't compromised. If it is a pass to my left, as you can see opposite, I put my right foot forward to give myself options.

However, if I'm running and want to pass right, and prepare for a pass with my right foot forward, I have two problems.

First my body position makes it difficult to continue running straight and still be able to make the pass backwards. With my right foot leading, the right side of my body and my right shoulder automatically lean forward, meaning I am passing across my chest and over my leg. I'm easy to hit because I am twisted and won't be presenting a strong body position and, worse still, I can't easily pass through the channel I talked about earlier – because it is blocked by the right shoulder and right leg. In order to make the pass easier from this position, I am likely to turn my body towards the recipient and take steps across the field. This cuts down my fellow attacker's space and it also reduces the threat I pose to the defender who is covering me because he will be able to follow me across the pitch and help his next defender.

The second problem I have if I am about to pass with the wrong leg forward is that I will be cutting down my options dramatically which is always a bad thing. You want to keep as many options open as possible at all times. It creates doubt in the mind of your opponents and that gives you an advantage. For instance, if you are passing right, off your right foot, you will tend to stop and pivot to create the space needed, as I described earlier. But

that's no good if you're trying to throw a dummy, because if you are twisted like that you've then got no forward momentum – so even if the dummy works, where are you going to go?

So getting the technique for short passing spot on is hugely important to keep the defence guessing. As the play unfolds around you, you might want to sell a dummy, or you might need to make your pass go a bit further, to miss out an opponent or a fellow attacker in order to create confusion and space in the defensive line. By establishing good technique and body position, all the passes look exactly the same and are very difficult to read from a defensive point of view.

In terms of actually releasing the pass, it is important that you draw the defender in by trying to turn his chest towards you. By this I mean that when the defender is directly in front of you, attack back at what we call his inside shoulder. To clarify, your inside shoulder and the defender's inside shoulder are both on the side from which you received the

**Passing to my left, my right foot is forward and my right elbow is up and vice versa**

pass, i.e. the pass comes in to you from the left – so your inside shoulder is your left shoulder and the defender's inside shoulder is his right shoulder.

So, as illustrated above, if an attacker receives a ball from the right he should run at the defender's left shoulder (i.e. the attacker runs right), and then pass out to his left (the defender's right), making it very difficult for the defender to change direction and defend against the pass. If I get the ball from the left I would attack back on the defender's right shoulder.

In rugby sometimes the best running lines take you across the field and can be sideways in nature. This can create confusion in defences and can highlight miss matches. The movement towards the inside shoulder of the defender is still massively key in preserving

the receiver's space and allowing him to run an equally effective line or exploit the indecision caused. This means that if you are running across the field (right to left) and want to pass in the same direction (left), it is very important to step in towards the defender, and if possible his inside shoulder, with your right foot (thus straightening your running line) just before giving the pass. Failing to do this will send the defenders on to the recipient, because of the lack of threat posed by the passer; but doing this well can cause late changes in angles of running lines from supporting players that can completely destroy good defences.

# There are no set rules. Keeping the move alive is what is important.

Above, the attacker with the ball should be aiming to run at the defender's right shoulder, to pull him away from the second attacker who will be receiving the pass. Instead, the first attacker is heading towards the defender's left shoulder so that when he releases the pass, the defender will actually be facing the second attacker, giving him much more chance of making a tackle or getting in the attacker's way

If the attacker is passing out to his right and he attacks the defender's left shoulder instead, the defender's chest remains in an open position, so the pass is easy to chase. The defender's momentum will be driving in the direction of the pass, meaning that he can still defend me until I pass and then carry on towards my team mate who now has the ball. Also, because I haven't taken my defender out of the game, the defence will, in effect, have an extra man and can shift one of their players further out to cover any over-laps. In a nutshell, I will have given the defender the opportunity to close down the space I want my team mate to be moving into.

What I've just been describing is, of course, the ideal passing technique. The reality is that no situation on the pitch is perfect and although it is very important that you master these basic principles of passing, it is also important that you realise you will have to manufacture passes from many less than ideal positions which may mean leg positions and elbow positions become irrelevant. In those circumstances, there are no set rules. Keeping the move alive is what is important.

## Practice drills

Ensuring that the basics of the short pass are second nature to you is critical. And getting used to quickly receiving and passing the ball on, keeping your technique solid and tight as I've described, is a vital skill. A great drill to practise both these elements can be easily set up. A line of players all ready to pass in the same direction with the correct foot forward and elbow up creating the channel, pass the ball up along the line and then change to pass back down – with penalties for incorrect technique. This could be a timed race where accuracy and technique can make all the difference. Great fun, but most of all, it helps quick, proper hands become second nature.

It is also important to practise the attacking moves I've described: making sure that you know how to turn your defender, set your leading foot correctly etc. You can do this by setting up a 2-on-1 or a 3-on-2 situation. One or two of your team mates act as defenders and two or three of you run towards them, bearing in mind everything I've been talking about. The 'defenders' try to mark the attackers whilst the player with the ball practises setting his body position correctly to draw the first defender and pass so that the second attacker can also then draw his defender and passes out to the third attacker who is then away up the field. Easy. Well, if you practise enough it can be. And once you have cracked that, you can mix things up with dummies, longer passes etc. This basic manoeuvre forms the core of many attacking strategies, as you will see. So getting it right is very important.

Above is a typical 3-on-2 situation that makes for a very good practice drill. The player with the ball attacks the defender's right shoulder, turning him in, before releasing the pass to his right. The second defender would then move across to the new player with the ball and the passing skill would be repeated

## Spin passing – how to do it

The hand position for spin passing or long passing is not massively different from the hand position for a short pass, but then it shifts slightly. For a pass out to your right, drop the left hand further down towards the base of the ball and the lower end point, and keep the right hand further up. In the pass itself, the left hand does all the work and the right hand is a guide.

There is still the same shape for the pass with the channel created by the elbow but, in addition, the left hand rotates over the top as the ball is released and the right hand guides. This creates the spinning motion which allows the ball to travel more quickly for a longer pass.

Again, same thing as the short passing, push through to the target. So the hands do exactly the same thing, except I'm now spinning the ball as I pass.

For a pass out to your left, your right hand drops lower down towards the base and the

left hand guides. The right hand moves over the top of the ball during the pass.

The important thing is to keep the nose of the ball slightly up. If the nose of the ball is slightly up, it means the ball will spin properly and you can pass to the target. If the nose is kept down, the ball stays in that position and you'll throw the ball downwards. It also spins with the nose in an odd position which is difficult to get your hands round. No one is going to catch one of those!

HOW TO PLAY RUGBY MY WAY

## Pitfalls

Not being aware of the weight of the pass to a team mate. If you get it wrong it can make his/her job very difficult. For example too soft a pass will not allow enough time to catch the ball and make a decision.

## Top tip

Practice is critical as you develop your passing skills. Until you have become totally confident with the skill you must always assess the risk of each pass. Throwing an unrealistic pass that you are not ready to take on, and thereby losing the ball at the wrong moment, can be dangerous.

# Your enjoyment grows the more success you have.

## Spin passing in action

The distance the ball is in the air, and the time the ball is in the air means that this pass is not used as close to the defensive line as short passes are. If I am right up against the defence and I throw a long pass, by the time the ball gets to my team mate his defender will be on him. So long spin passes are most effective when you are attacking slightly further away from the defence unless, as was mentioned before, the recipient is in open space. It is then vital to make the defence commit to other attackers being missed by the pass; thus the ball is taken right up to the defence, before being released.

Too many people when they spin a pass will stop, pivot and wind up a big pass. This of course telegraphs the intention, and lets a defender move off the passing player and head across to the intended recipient. That's no good. Remember, stopping and committing a member of the defence gives you an advantage. So, although it is not as imperative as it is for short passes, it is still very important that you work off your leading left leg for a pass out to the right, and vice versa. This enables you to threaten the defence before throwing the long pass, or throw a dummy and keep moving.

The spin on the ball helps it travel further, but if for instance, you are throwing a long, miss pass (i.e. you are deliberately missing the team mate next to you, throwing across the front of him – while he runs a good attacking line – to a wider player further away, to create more space) you need to combine the spin with strength. This tends to come from your abdominal area, what I call your core area (i.e. round your waist). With your technique in place you can really pull your arms through in the pass with your chest following the movement – this gives momentum and strength to the extra long pass and means you can throw the pass without having to run too much in the same direction that the ball will travel.

## *Practice drills*

A good drill is just simply passing balls around between players. Simple I know, but what you are looking out for is to see not only how the ball feels, but also how well the ball span and whether it reached its intended target or not. It is all about getting comfortable with the ball in hand, setting your posture correctly and unleashing the pass as fluently and naturally as possible.

Another excellent drill is to carry out a set of ten passes, the aim being 'How accurate can I be with all ten passes?' Another drill would be a set of ten passes with a catch and then a pass. How accurate and how fast can these be executed? Both of these drills can be used with a stopwatch and can be really enjoyable.

In coaching terms what you are looking for in order to assess whether it is a good pass or a bad pass, is whether the fingers themselves are spread on the ball, and if the hands are pushing the ball through with the fingers pointing to the target.

Another drill is again back to that 3-on-2 situation I discussed on page 51. To use the long pass the first attacker can take the ball towards the defending line and use a miss pass across the second attacker, out to the

**Keeping the ball away from the body as you catch it accurately means it can be passed on quickly**

## Catching

third attacker in space. Get used to seeing the situation unfold and making it happen. It is vital that the first attacker takes the ball right up to the defence, forcing the two defenders to make a decision – they will have to commit to two of the attackers, leaving the third man free.

Also, get used to reading whether the second defender is committed or whether he is drifting on to the third attacker. Learn when and how to change the longer spin pass into a shorter pass for the second attacker who is now in the space.

It is all very well your team mates firing over the perfect pass to you, with space around in which to launch a match-winning attack, if all you do is drop the ball when it gets to you. Or even if you do gather it in, if the situation demands that you feed it out instantly to a team mate and you end up dithering with it in your hands, again, the game could be lost in that split second.

So, another important factor in passing the ball is catching it. When the ball is on its way towards you, always have your hands spread in the air, facing the ball, as a target for your team mate to aim at. When the ball comes, try

and catch it in the manner in which you wish to hold it in order to pass it. If you achieve that, it can give you that one moment's advantage which might be vital. Catching may seem simple, but it is amazing how much better we all can be at catching by focusing on the basics that we take for granted.

Everything – the shoulders, hands, etc. – should be manoeuvered around the ball. If you simply catch it in the chest or any old how in the hands, this will mean you have to adjust your position and handling in order to be able to pass the ball on. This takes time and can sometimes be the difference between scoring and not scoring. Try to watch the ball on its way in and get your hands around it by tilting the shoulders, manoeuvring the hands and reacting to the way the ball is flying. This means the next pass can be performed quickly and perfectly. You'll be ready for it.

## Practice drill

A good drill to practise catching is again a simple one. Your team should line up in a long line and pass along the line, each person trying to present a target, catch the ball in the right way and move it on down the line as quickly and effectively as possible. Try timing yourselves and then try to beat your best time.

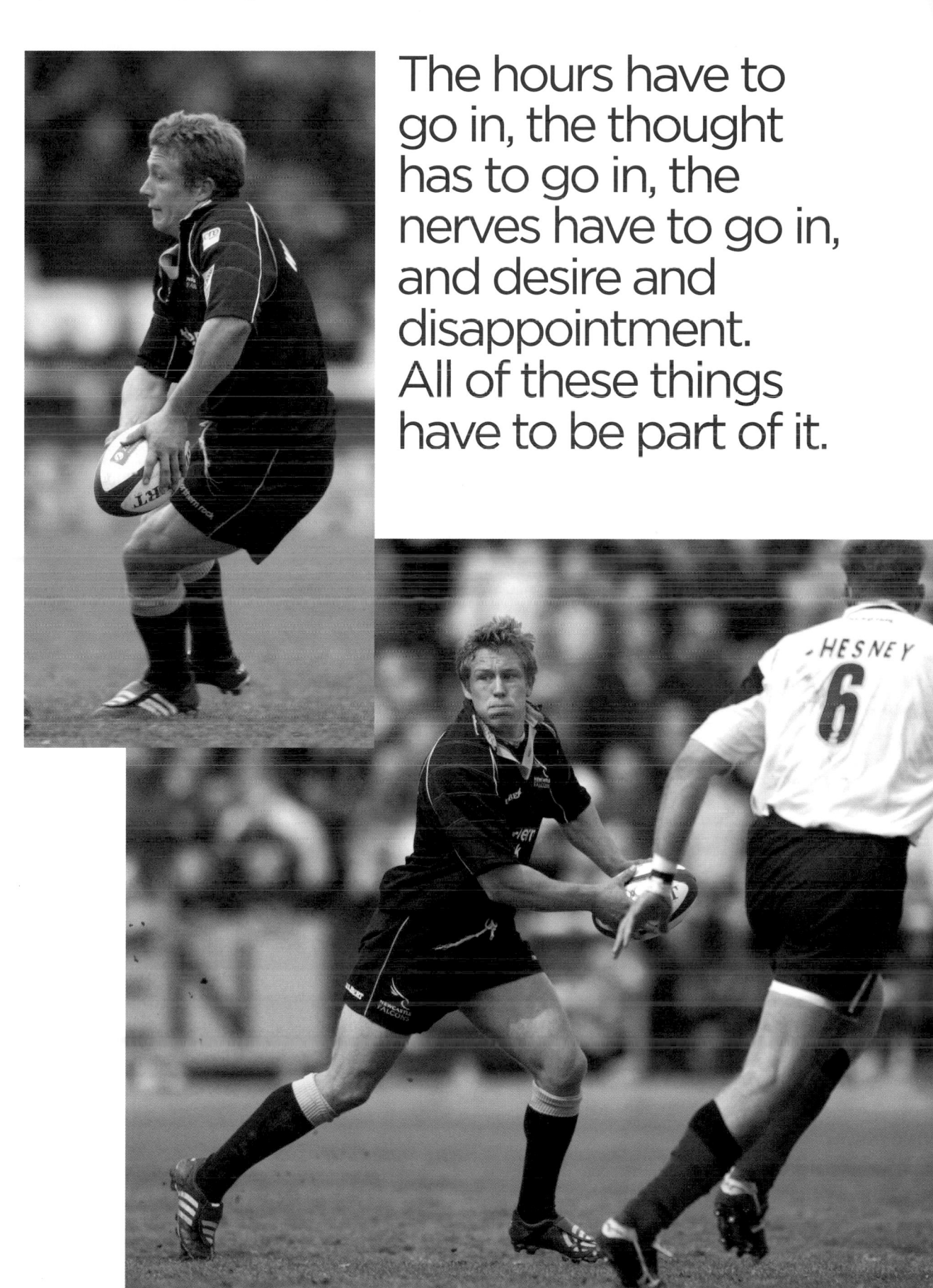

The hours have to go in, the thought has to go in, the nerves have to go in, and desire and disappointment. All of these things have to be part of it.

**Top tip**

Learn how to move the ball to a team mate when it is not possible to have both hands available. Practise playing with a ball on your own; gripping it with one hand, moving it around your back and passing accurately in any fashion. Mastering this skill may be the difference between scoring a try or having to go to ground and set the ball up where the ball may be challenged and turned over.

## Offloading

This is used when an attacker is about to be brought down, but wants to ensure that his team retains possession of the ball without having to create a ruck situation (that is when the ball is on the ground and one or more players from each team are contesting for it, while on their feet). It is not an exact science and will depend on how the situation you are in develops.

To start off with there are two ways you can carry the ball which should give you the chance to move it on if tackled: you can carry the ball slightly out from your body, with two hands, which allows you to threaten, dummy, or to pass when tackled; the other option is to carry the ball close to your chest with one

hand, which allows you to use your other hand as a fend-off against tackling. Both of these positions allow for an offload.

Carrying the ball with two hands give you plenty of options when it comes to off-loading. Imagine you have, using good footwork and agility, managed to skip between two defenders, and have forced a low tackle to stop you. If you are holding the ball with two hands it is possible to lift the ball over the top of the tackler and pass backwards. Or if the defender isn't tackling you low, but is looking to smother you, you have the flexibility of shifting the ball to one hand, ready for an under arm offload if a support runner has followed you through the defensive line.

Consider this situation when carrying the ball with one hand. You are attacking with a team mate on your right hand side and two defenders are coming at you (basically a 2-on-2). The first defender on the left comes towards you, so you hold the ball with your right hand, attack the space outside him and use your left to fend him off. Then the second defending player on the right comes in and tackles or is about to complete the tackle on you. Now you can use a one-hand offload to pass the ball back through behind you to your team mate on the right, without having to use your left hand, which might be pinned down or engaged in fending off the defender. This type of offload is very difficult to read. Confusing the defence again because it is completely untelegraphed. For this to be most effective, you need to be able to perform it with both hands. That will take a bit of work – but it is worth it. And no surprise – this is known as the one-hand offload. Clever. This technique may be a little more

difficult for younger players who lack the strength in the wrists and the forearms, but it is still worth considering practising, if not using in game play just yet.

Having to off-load the ball doesn't necessarily mean you have actually been tackled. It might be that you are just about to be and you need to react quickly. For instance, you should be able to catch a ball, even above your head, and get rid of it straight away. If you catch the ball high and you haven't got time to bring it down, create the channel and pass with the perfect technique, you mustn't think, 'Oh, I can't get rid of it.' Your reaction has to be: 'Where are my team mates?' 'How can I keep this attack moving?' 'How do I get the ball to them?' It is all about practising handling the ball in different ways so that you become comfortable with a variety of ways of passing and can adapt and react to situations, which again can be the difference between winning and losing.

HOW TO PLAY RUGBY MY WAY

## *Practice drills*

There is no specific practice drill that can cover all the scenarios that might develop in a game and in which you will want to off-load the ball. What is most important is that you get used to playing around with the ball in your hands. How it feels, how it moves, how you can move it. You can then utilise all the little tricks you develop yourself in actual game play. It can make all the difference.

A few ideas to get you started. Grip the top of the ball in one hand, release it, then grab it quickly with that same hand again – over and over. Or work with a partner and just see if you can throw the ball to your partner with a one-handed grip, but with more overhead movement perhaps, or behind your back. When you're passing back and forth, see if you can catch with one hand and pass it back. Catch it higher and lower and at different areas around your body. Try it with your left hand as well (if you are right-handed, or vice versa). And also try spinning the ball from one hand to the other. Basically, just mess around with the ball and invent your own tricks. Getting used to handling it is what it is all about. Not all passes are perfect, so reacting to high and low balls is extremely useful.

## Top tip

One way to strengthen your wrists and forearms in order to be able to off-load the ball one handed is to use squeezing grips. These are two plastic handles, joined in a V-shape, with a spring at the open end for resistance. So if you're sitting in front of the TV, you can just alternate hands and play with the grips.

# Best in the business

For mixing long and short passes as well as all-round handling ability, both Matthew Gidley (right) and Andrew Johns (far right) from the Australian NRL are exceptional.

For long spin passes, it has got to be Graeme Bachop of New Zealand.

HOW TO PLAY RUGBY MY WAY

**Skills**
# Tackling

# Tackling

**T**ackling is about stopping your opponent. The two most important things when you're tackling are: one, to get the opponent on the floor as quickly as possible, stopping his forward momentum, and two, to stop the ball. As the defensive team, the last thing you want to do is to let the ball get through your line.

Obviously if you can dislodge the ball in a tackle, you can create more opportunities. For example if you're going to tackle someone and you aim at the area around the ball, in an 'offensive' tackle, and you hit them in that area, you've a better chance of dislodging the ball. That's great, but your primary goal should always be about stopping that attacker from going forward, and then, as a secondary aim for the team, stopping the attacker off-loading the ball to one of his own players.

If I make a tackle and the attacker is toppling over, the important thing for a second defender to do is to try and wrap up the ball. That stops the attacker off-loading and it means your team has a chance of winning the ball back. But as the first defender in this situation, I must always remember my primary goal is to stop my opponent and low tackles are the most effective way of achieving that aim – they take away the attacker's momentum and leg drive, putting them on the floor. That's my job; leave the second defender to work on the ball if he can. Tackling and focusing on the ball area when an attacker is in space is dangerous and leaves the attacker able to use footwork and handoffs to evade the defender, who will be in too much of an upright position and easily deceived.

Common to both styles of defence – low and ball tackles – is perhaps the most important element of the whole skill: focus.

73

## Focus

Low tackling is the most effective way of getting your man on the floor. So you have to focus on a specific area of the legs, and focus intensely. For ball tackles, when you are wanting to stop the ball as well as the attacker, the focus is just as intense, but this time it is on and around your opponent's waist, so that you'll be making impact around where the ball is. As I've said, that's important for dislodging and stopping the ball in its tracks.

Focus helps you make a successful tackle. Think of the analogy of a rampaging elephant. If it's charging at you and you pull out a gun and shoot in the general direction of the elephant, you're less likely to do any damage than if you specifically aim for its eye or its heart. This is the same idea. If someone's coming at

you with the ball, and you see them as a whole person (i.e. you are looking at the big picture rather than the specific detail), you're more likely to get fended off, knocked over or deceived by them, because you are flooding your brain with too much information for it to be precise and accurate in performing the skill. But if you cut out the excess and just focus on a point at the thigh, just above the knee, or at the waist, on the ball, then you have a far greater chance of stopping them in their tracks.

## Pitfalls

**Not having a specific focus or target impact area to aim at as you set yourself for the tackle.**

## Low tackling – how to do it

When you are about to make this type of
tackle on your opponent's legs, the first point
is to think low, with an intense focus on where
you are about to hit. Next point is that you
don't just bend at the waist to get lower.
Instead you bend your knees and drop your
hips so that you're semi-squatting, giving you
a strong posture that allows you to power
through the tackle while keeping your back
straight, almost at a 90 degree angle with
your legs, and keeping your head up – maintaining your focus for as long as possible.

Obviously you will be bent a little at the waist
in this stance but now your shoulders, back,
waist and legs all form a strong line of resistance. The third point is to drive your shoulder
into the part of your opponent that you're
focusing on (i.e. the point just above the
knee).

## Top tip

Go low when there is space to cover, you don't have support and you are faced with an opponent with good footwork who is capable of deceiving you. Keeping your feet moving and tackling low around the legs eliminates this threat.

## Head-on tackles

To demonstrate these points, consider a head-on tackle. If I've got someone running at me and I want to make a right shoulder tackle, my head goes to the left of their legs so that I take their full weight on my right shoulder and the right side of my chest and their momentum carries them over the top of my right shoulder. Obviously for a left shoulder tackle, my head goes to the right and then again, the full weight over the top of my left shoulder.

One of the key points is to continue working your feet through the hit. This is so you don't wait for the attacker, standing there with planted feet. If you do that, you will take on their full weight when contact is made and you'll be driven backwards. Not exactly what you had planned. It might even be worse than that – you might not make any sort of tackle

Standing waiting for the attacker to get to you, with feet rooted to the ground, a lack of focus on where you are going to hit, and a weak body position can have disastrous consequences – as Sparks happily demonstrates here

at all. If your opponent is running at you and you are standing there with your feet planted, the attacker may change direction. If that happens, you've got no way of following them as you will be rooted to the spot. You are going to look pretty silly. So keep your feet light and fast. You see a lot of American football players doing quick feet drills when they're warming up. Lots of running on the spot to stay light footed.

You can also make your tackle more effective by continuing to drive the legs into the hit. If you don't, and lunge into a head-on tackle, and the person you're tackling puts their forearm out as a shield, as soon as you hit that arm you're going to drop to the floor because you've got no drive. If, however, you continue to move forward with your legs, and even once you've made the hit, you continue to drive with your legs, and your opponent tries to hand you off, you will go bursting through

the defensive block and still make the tackle. Continuing your leg drive also helps you to get your feet as close as possible to the attacker. This means you can drive your shoulder in with more impact. If you are caught reaching because you are too far away, you will end up making the impact with only your bicep or lower arm. This will create a weak impact and will cause injury as well as being easily evaded or powered through by the attacker.

HOW TO PLAY RUGBY MY WAY

Of course your opponent will also have his legs moving – he's likely to be running full pelt at you. So somehow you've got to negate that momentum and power – that is why it is essential when you make the hit with your shoulder that you wrap your arms tightly around his legs so that the combination of shoulders and arms takes his leg drive out of the equation. This will help to ensure that your opponent goes to the floor.

## Top tip

The skill of getting back on your feet quickly when in the process of making a tackle is very important. As a defender, this allows you to challenge for the ball, quickly and effectively. You can achieve this by using your opponent's momentum or body to swing up onto two feet with a wide base to stabilise you, and get your hands on the ball. We use this technique because the tackler can play the ball in a tackle situation without worrying about being offside as long as he is on his feet. Getting up quickly also helps you work back into the defensive line to add strength and support to your team defence.

## Side-on tackles

Consider now a side-on tackle. The key points are the same as for the head-on tackle: for a right shoulder tackle, the head goes to the left; for a left shoulder tackle, head to the right; and again, you will need to focus intensely on hitting low. But here, even more so than with a head-on tackle, you must continue to drive your legs. Remember, this is a side-on tackle, so if someone is running away from you, and you lunge, as soon as you leave the floor in what might look a spectacular dive, the hand-off is likely to render you completely useless; flapping at thin air. Because you are coming in from the side, you don't have your own body acting as a block right in front of the attacker. If, however, you are still working your legs, he can try to hand you off

## Pitfalls

**Lunging into a tackle from a distance without driving the legs. Flapping at thin air never brought anyone down.**

# There is a huge desire to make the most of whatever time I've got in the game.

but you can continue to drive through that, make it to the tackle and create a big tackle with your shoulder. And always remember to wrap your arms around your opponent's legs. You want them to hit the deck. A lot of people making tackles don't wrap their arms tightly enough, so the attacker can pull their foot away and escape.

So, to sum up, focus low and intensely on where you are aiming to make the hit, drop your hips, get your feet close, drive your legs (in particular if you are coming in from the side), stay light on your feet, lots of foot contact, drive your shoulder in, head to the right or the left, make a big impact, and finally wrap your arms tightly around the legs.

## Ball tackling

Tackling above the shoulders is illegal and dangerous and can result in serious injury. It is poor technique, a lazy execution and totally unprofessional.

The point of low tackles is to get the man on the floor. As I have said, that is the primary aim of a tackle – but it might not mean that your team retrieves the ball, and it might not even put a complete stop to the attack, as the ball may still be alive. For instance, as I described in the Passing chapter, the attacker may manage to off-load as you make the tackle. Sometimes, however, it is possible to tackle and stop the ball as well. In these cases we use a ball tackle, as defined above. Ball tackles tend to come into play when you are

defending with support on your inside and outside, and the attacker running at you has nowhere else to go and doesn't have lots of footwork (so it's not Jason Robinson!). In those circumstances, the attacker's options are limited – he is going to have to run directly at you.

The basics are the same as for a low tackle. You've got to focus again on the one spot you want to hit – just above the waist this time and just under the ball – but the difference here is that you drive from low to high with your shoulder, your legs and your back. What is critical is that you keep a very straight back, and you hit the attacker rising up through the tackle (i.e. you power into the tackle and hit up and through your opponent like an aeroplane taking off, using the strength of your back and especially your legs).

For a ball tackle your back should be angled at 45 degrees, driving forward. If you sit back over your heels without driving your legs and moving into the tackle, your centre of gravity is going to go backwards. That's no good. If you try and make the tackle with a slightly bent back and without bending your knees or dipping, you're going to get hit in a weak position, and crumble over your bent legs on to your backside. Definitely no good. However, if you're in a low position with a straight back, it doesn't matter if the other player tries to put more pressure on you, they're going to drive their weight through the straight line of your back and legs and you will be in a strong enough position to send his power back through him.

Standing waiting to tackle Sparks with my centre of gravity falling backwards, and in a weak position; kind of embarrassing, I won't do that again

There are two specialist pointers to keep in mind with this tackle. The first is how you use your arms, and it is different from the wrapping in a low tackle. Here you are making contact above the legs so you try to use one of your arms to hook a leg, rather than wrapping both around. You hit the tackle with your shoulder and hook a leg with the opposite arm. By lifting that leg, it takes away the attacker's stability and leg drive as well as shifting his centre of gravity, which means that you can tip them over easily. This is obviously an aggressive tackle, but it's very effective if done well. But it is quite a technical move and has to be worked on to get it right. The other arm wraps around the body or grasps hold of the shirt.

Secondly, if you do what we call 'beating the opponent to the tackle', you can knock them backwards. By this I mean if the attacker's running into you and sees you standing still, he knows where the point of impact will be, he can get his foot down into a strong position and brace himself for the hit. However if he thinks you're going to meet him at a certain spot, and you accelerate at the last moment and meet him closer, then he hasn't got time to prepare. When you hit him, he may go backwards which is why we talk about accelerating through the hit. And it's a great feeling when it works. Not only does it stop the attack dead in its tracks but seeing an opponent rocked backwards like that is a huge morale boost for the whole team. I love it.

## Practice drills

A good description for establishing effective practice drills of tackling is 'little and often'. It is hard work and should be organised in short segments which the brain can handle. For instance, a set might be three low tackles using your right shoulder, then three on the

left or it could be a variety of highs and lows, from the side and from in front. However you organise it, you must focus on being precise – this allows you to concentrate properly and process the information so you make meaningful gains in the improvement of this skill. Don't focus on how many repetitions you can do, but instead think about how well you can do each in the set and how confident you feel.

If you have them, tackle bags are great for practising. A particularly good drill is to have someone drag the bag behind them as quickly as possible, and then you can practise your side-on, low tackles by hitting the bag in the correct manner. Or you can use a stationary tackle bag with a partner in place to pick it up and reset it. Now you hit it and get to your feet – and challenge for the imaginary ball. Then back off to the line five yards away before repeating. A set of six tackles on each shoulder is great practice and can improve your game-related fitness.

HOW TO PLAY RUGBY MY WAY

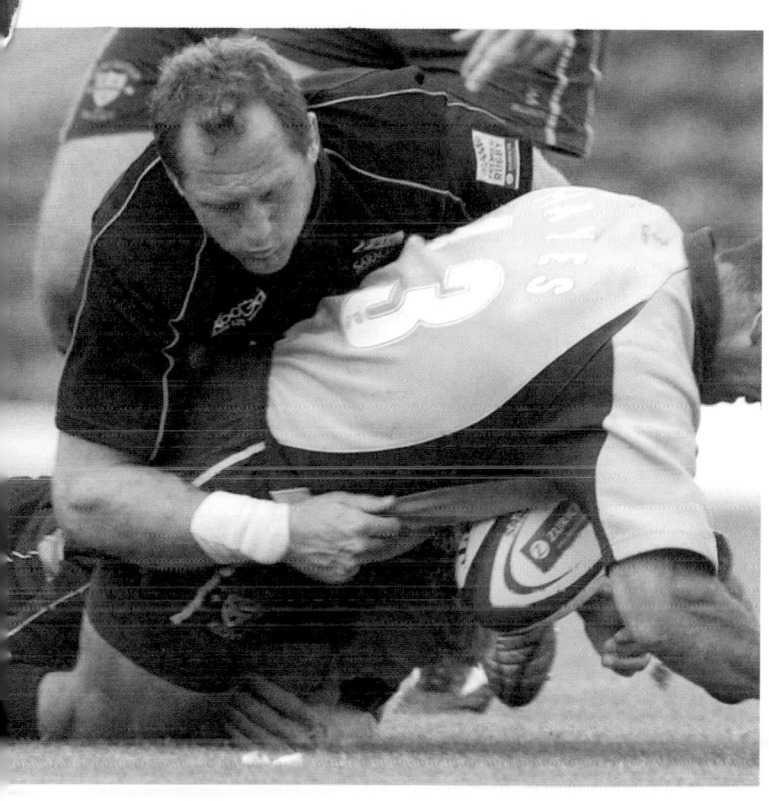

# Best in the business

Richard Hill of England. He does not always put in massive hits, but he rarely misses a tackle, and is incredibly fast back on to his feet with a work rate to die for. Team mates love a player like that.

Brian Lima of Samoa is the hardest tackler I've ever faced. Not surprisingly, he's known as 'The Chiropractor' because he makes your bones shake when he hits you. His technique is very strong, but it's also the sheer pace with which he attacks his tackles. You'll turn round and suddenly he's coming in from your blind side. There's nothing you can do, and you know all about it when the impact comes.

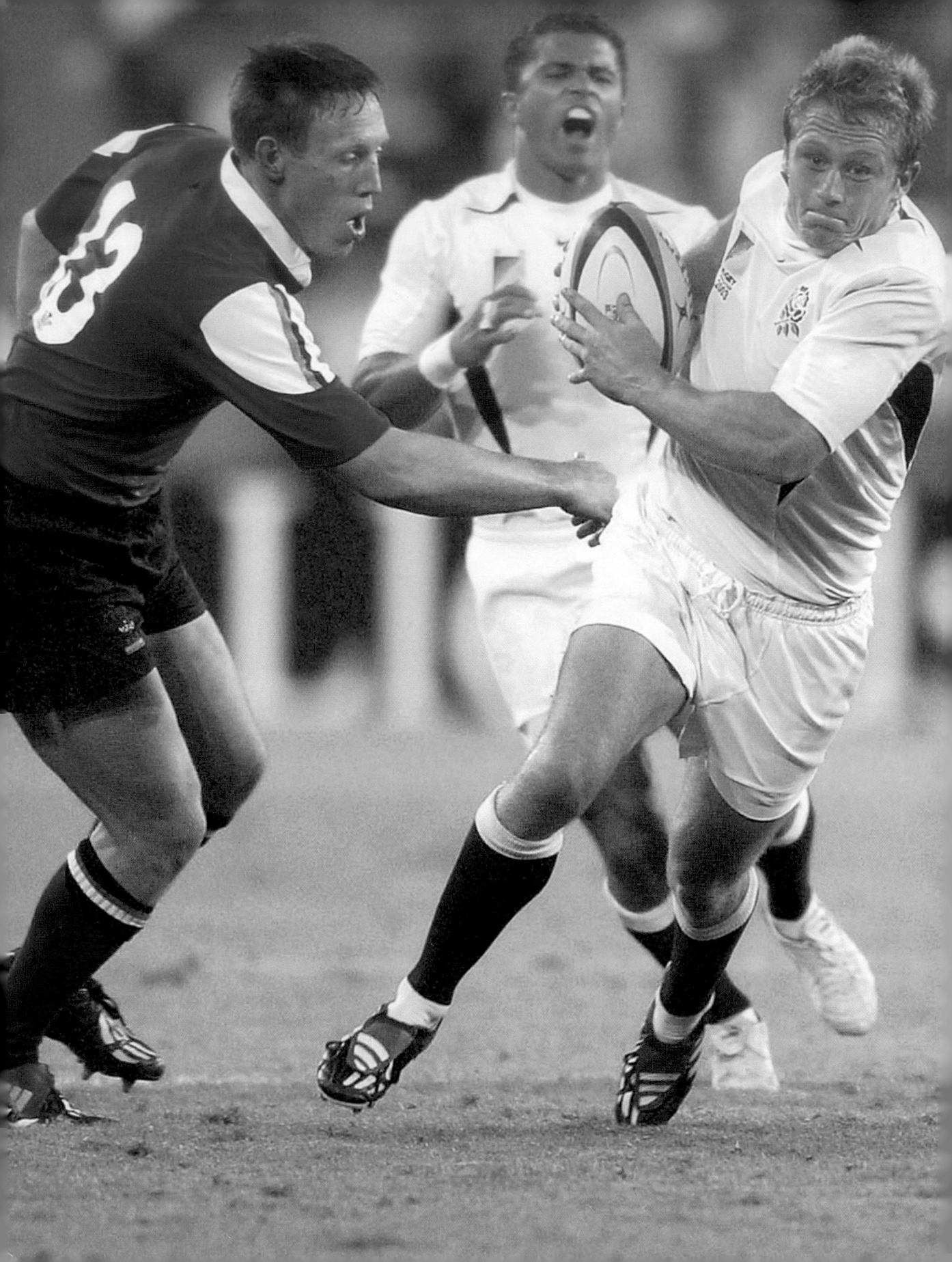

# Skills
# Attacking

# Attacking

I n the chapter on passing I discussed the technical aspects of how to pass, catch and off-load. I also touched on some of the attacking scenarios that can unfold in game play and in which the ability to pass correctly can make all the difference. But there is more to successful attacking play than passing – here I will expand on how to develop and successfully execute those attacking opportunities.

## Space

The first and most important point in mounting an attack is to ensure that space on the pitch is preserved. You want to make sure you stop the defenders from encroaching into those areas that your fellow attackers can utilise. Moving into space means you can move forward, and that's what it is all about. So, when you are attacking with the ball, and a defender approaches you to make the tackle, there will generally be space on either side. That is the space you need to preserve for your supporting players to run into.

When faced with a 3-on-3 situation you should always see four spaces rather than three defenders. Preserving this space is why I was so specific in the passing chapter about making sure you lead with your right leg for a

# Training makes me feel stronger, more capable and I can attack any situation that's ahead of me.

pass off your right hand out to your left, and lead with your left leg for a pass off your left hand out to the right. Once you have mastered that technique, it will allow you to preserve that all-important space. So here is the scene. I am moving towards a defender with the ball in my hand and I am aware that my team mate is in the space to my right. What I must make sure I don't do is run across the field into my fellow attacker's space, as the ball carrier is doing in the above diagram. If I do that all I will achieve is to drag the defender with me, because he will follow my movement in an attempt to make his tackle on me. If that happens, he will be occupying the space I was intending to preserve for my team mate – the diagram on the right shows how the defender is now in that space.

Attacking the defender's inside shoulder means he will have to turn away from the supporting team mate in order to attempt to make the tackle on the ball carrier. This will preserve space for the second attacker to move into once he receives the ball

So crabbing across the pitch here is not a good option. Instead, I can either run straight and attack the defender using some of the footwork and agility skills I will discuss later in this chapter or, even better, I can move towards the defender and hold him (by interesting and threatening him) or, better still, pull him to the left, away from the side where I want the space to be preserved. So, if my fellow attacker is steaming up on my right, what I do is move to my left, in effect back towards the defender's inside shoulder, which we discussed in the Passing chapter on page 49. Think of it as aiming to stop the defender from moving towards the player I am passing to. This manoeuvre will mean that the defender has to stop and check his movement or, even better, turn into me to try and make his challenge – his chest will be angled away from the space I intend to pass into and where my team mate will receive the ball and

progress forward unimpeded. The fact that I will be leading with my left leg forward when I make the pass means that I will have room to my right to get the ball away – before the defender hits me of course. If I was leading with my right leg forward and the defender was closing in on me there would be far less room to make the pass – and a greater chance that I will fluff it or the defender will get his hands on the ball.

If you execute this correctly there is no way the defender can get back across to try and halt my fellow attacker. Even if he smashes into me and knocks me out of the way, the pass will already have been made and his momentum will take him in the wrong direction. My team mate will be off and running into huge space or at least with an opportunity to attack inside or outside his defender.

# Don't give up, be the best you can be, reach your potential.

The movements I have just described may also open up another option. If a defender decides not to commit to you, and instead continues to drift left in the situation I have just described, towards the space my fellow attacker is heading for, I can then dummy a pass and continue to run. With my left leg forward when I dummy the pass to my right, I will have all the momentum I need to speed through the gap the defender will have left. What is really important, however, is that you don't stop to pivot before the dummy. If the defender drifts off and I stop to pivot and look like I am about to pass it, but then take the opportunity to dummy, I can't attack that gap

because I'll be stuck with planted feet. So, once again being able to pass with the correct leg leading is very important, or if that's not possible, then maintaining forward momentum is vital.

If I want to preserve the space on my left (the defender's right), it is the opposite of the scene I have just described. I move in towards the defender's inside shoulder (left) and stop him or pull him to the right, away from the space I want to preserve. I try to make sure my right leg is leading and I pass out to my left. Got him again.

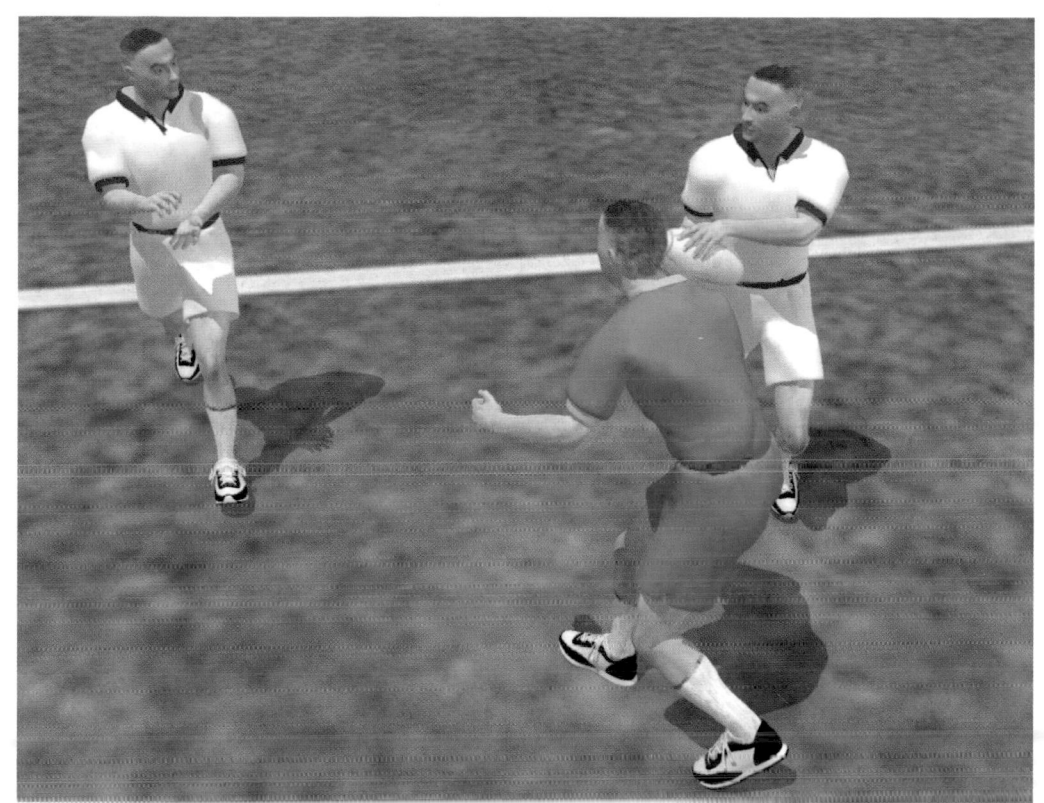

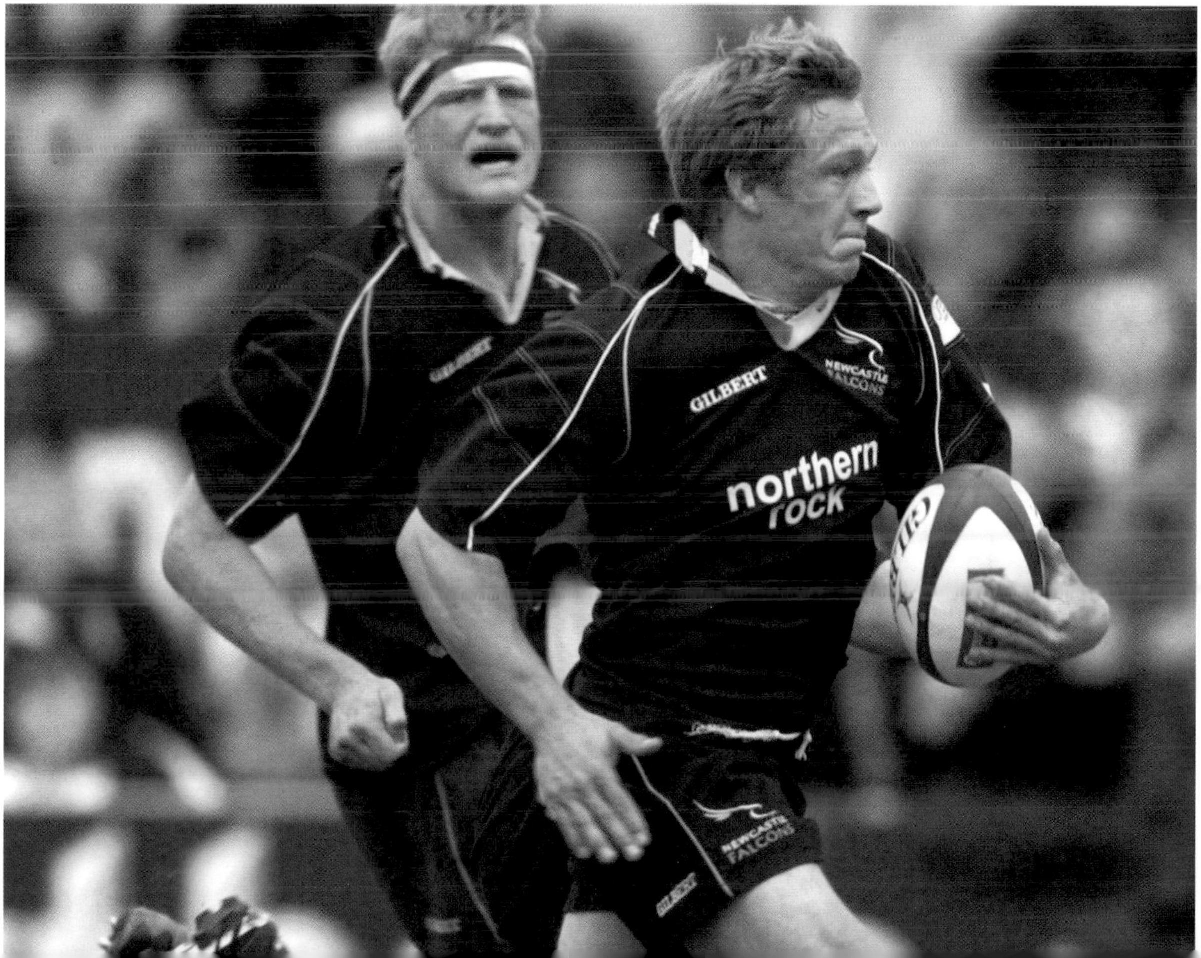

GILBERT
NEWCASTLE FALCONS
northern rock

## Communication

In attacking play, one of the biggest points is communication. Nothing ever gets done unless it gets said first; nobody knows what's going on unless you tell them what's going on. The more information you can give a team mate in an instant, the better the decision they can make. It's amazing how important this is.

For example, if I'm about to give a pass to someone and they tell me that they're running a short line on me, that they're deep, that they want the ball soft and they want it right now, I can think, 'Short, deep, yeah, right now, right now.' I know exactly what I'm supposed to do.

If someone tells me, 'Fix your man, fix your man and then give it to me short,' I again know what I need to do. If I am looking for the ball to come to me immediately, because my team mate is about to be tackled by a flying defender I will shout, 'Get it out of your hands.' Things like this can prove critical. 'Miss me out, miss me out, miss me out,' or 'Give it to me, give it to me'; these sorts of comments are fantastic. The thing to remember is don't be afraid to let yourself be heard when you have to, don't be embarrassed – the best players are the most talkative. If you want the ball you have to ask for it.

## Depth

Another key point in attacking moves is depth. As we've just seen, with a 2-on-1 (two attackers and one defender), your aim as the attacker is to draw the defender to you, then give the ball to your team mate who can then go free. In that situation, we need very little depth. If I'm running a 2-on-1, and there is a space for my fellow attacker to move into, I'd expect him to be quite flat on me (i.e. almost parallel with me – not far behind). This is because when the defender commits to tackle me, and at that moment I give the ball to my team mate, by the time that team mate takes possession of that ball at pace and goes,

the defender will be held for a moment and even if the defender did manage to turn and get away from the tackle and regroup in an attempt to get to the ball carrier, there is no chance. My team mate will be long gone with the ball.

If, however, I draw the defender and I pass the ball back to a team mate too far behind me, the defender may have time to cover me, then move on and defend the second attacker. So being fairly shallow in such circumstances is the key to maintaining pace and penetration through the defence.

HOW TO PLAY RUGBY MY WAY

However, if we have a 3-on-2 situation (three attackers and two defenders), the depth required for the move changes, depending on the situation. If I'm the second attacker and I take the ball flat after my team mate has drawn the defender and laid it off to me, I won't have enough time to get my own pass away. The second defender will be too near to me – all over me and occupying my space, ready to tackle immediately as shown in these diagrams.

## Blackie's secrets

We do lots of work on stepping by people and swerving. Changing angle and pace at the same time and changing it at an optimal distance from the opponent, so you just get them off track. If you change too early, they'll be able to see it and catch you, or they'll readjust themselves if they're quite quick. Remember, at the top of the professional level, most players are quite quick, quite agile, so we need to keep working all the time on staying quicker and more agile.

In that situation, what I should have done is hold my depth as in the diagram above, understanding that I need to have enough time and space to get my pass away as well. So if I take the ball slightly further behind the ball carrier than I would in a 2-on-1 situation, I can catch it with my hands in the right position to pass it off, and I'll have time to draw my defender and put my third man away on the outside. That said, I need to make sure I am not too deep or stood still so that the first defender can move on to me and create a 2-on-2 (see right). It's important to be moving on to the ball so that if a gap appears in front of me I can accelerate through it. If a defender appears in front of me then I can take my foot off the gas – slow down – and create my own depth ready for a pass.

Engineering a miss pass can get you out of a tricky situation when you are sitting too flat

There is a way out of the situation if you find yourself too flat next to the ball carrier and you are 3-on-2 with the defence, as illustrated in these diagrams. If that happens you can look to draw your defender onto yourself, but this time you tell the ball carrier to miss you out. This is all about effective vocal decoy. If you're running the line in the middle, and you want to get missed out, you need to convince the defender you're going to get the ball. You can use eye contact, a big call, a bit of foot-work, anything you can to make him think you're taking him on. Then, as long as your team mate recognises whatever signals you should have previously worked out, when the defender comes to get you the ball goes across in front of you and out to the third attacker on the outside. It is in this situation that the spin pass comes into play to gener-ate distance. If the defender stays out then the second attacker accelerates on to the short pass through the gap.

Depth is also about recognising who you're playing with. If I'm playing with a fast player on my inside, and he's got the ball, what I don't want to do is stand too far away, because as he runs off with the ball, he's going to create even more depth. So if I stand fairly flat with him, as he accelerates away, that move will create its own depth. If he's a long way forward and I'm a long way back,

# If you work hard at your job and what you do, then you should be able to do whatever you want to.

we're going to have a big a distance between us that I won't be able to make up and I'm going to get left behind.

However, if I'm standing with a slower player then I might want to just stand a bit deeper and because I know I can catch him and create the necessary depth that way. So it's important you know who you're playing with. That's often another part of communication, being able to say 'Pull back, pull back, just hold a bit more, hold a bit more, hold a bit more,' or 'Come flat, come flat' or 'I'm flat' or 'I'm deep' or anything that lets your team mates know where you are.

So, to sum up, it is all about being aware of what possibilities might arise as the game unfolds and thinking about the depth and lines you need to run to exploit those possibilities to the maximum. When you're playing outside of very fast players, you might need to understand that they're going to be very good at getting around defenders and creating 2-on-1s from 2 on 2s, so you have to run the right lines. If you're playing with big strong attackers on your inside, and you know that they might be better at bursting through tackles to create the offload after the tackle, you'll have to change your support line to accommodate them.

## Threatening the defence

Before I pass the ball in virtually any attacking move, I must threaten the defence. That's one of the cardinal rules. As I said previously, drifting across the pitch without knowing what you are trying to achieve reduces the space available for your team mates to work in and it can also create the possibility of a two-man attack on the recipient of your pass if you have not taken your defender out of the game.

### 3-on-2s

I've already dealt with the depth aspects of the 3-on-2 situation, but attacking the defence is also very important. The key thing to think about in this respect is what spaces are available.

Picture the attacking move. Remember, it is two defenders, three spaces and three attackers. One defender is positioned on the inside of the first attacker, a second defender is positioned just inside the second attacker, and the final attacker is on the outside. What the attackers need to be doing is running into space, never running at a man (unless, that is, you are very confident that you have the footwork and agility to get around him when facing him head on or the strength to run over him).

Assuming that none of the three attackers is going to attempt to skip past one of the defenders, your attack can still make significant headway. Number 1 attacker should run at the inside of the first defender, and once that defender has been drawn to him he can pass to number 2 attacker who should be

running towards the space on the inside of the second defender. Number 2 attacker, who now has the ball, has two options, depending on how the defender he is running towards reacts. If the defender drifts out to try and tackle number 3 attacker, attacker number 2 can flatten up and accelerate on to the ball, through the hole that will be left by the defender's decision – as shown above.

If, however, the defender moves to tackle the ball carrier, the ball carrier should attack that defender's inside shoulder as I have discussed, draw the defender in and then pass out to number 3 who will be fairly shallow and in space ready for a short pass to put him away.

That's what happens when you attack the defence in the conventional way.

However, if the attackers run directly at the defenders (and again assuming that they don't have the footwork to skip past them), it becomes easier for the defenders to cover the head-long charge and also keep a half eye out for the pass because they won't be being pulled to one side. Their chests will remain pointing towards the next defender, meaning they can cover two players and there will be less space created for the attackers to move into. So the defender has a chance of either: covering attacker 1 and moving in time to challenge attacker 2 (who now has the ball); or, if number 2 attacker has been sitting too deep then the second defender can react to a call from defender 1 to leave attacker 2 for him and slide on to defend attacker 3.

HOW TO PLAY RUGBY MY WAY

# Pitfalls

**Crabbing across the field before passing which invites pressure and allows extra defenders to get to the receiver of the ball, who now has less space in which to attack.**

Also if you run directly at a man, you've now got no dummy option because the defender doesn't have to make a choice between covering the possible pass you might make, or going for you. By facing you directly, he can do both. If you try and dummy and hold onto the ball, you are likely to get smashed. The defender will still be there right in front of you. That's why it's important to run into space. It also means if the defence rushes up at the last minute you will be running at arms and not shoulders so you will be more difficult to tackle and stop. It will also be easier to off-load and keep the move flowing.

Exactly the same applies if you are executing a long, spinning miss pass as I described earlier. The running line for attacker 2 is still the space inside the second defender even if he is not actually going to receive the ball. That's attacking space, and not the defenders.

## *Switch and dummy switch*

The cardinal rule of attacking or threatening the defence applies even if I am planning a dummy switch manoeuvre, which actually requires me to run across the pitch.

A dummy switch is where I run diagonally across the pitch – say left to right – with the supposed intention of slipping a pass to a team mate who is running back into the space that I have run away from. That would be a normal switch move – the dummy occurs when I don't hand off the ball but instead hold on to it, hopefully causing confusion in the defence because the first defender sees my team mate coming back into his channel and he will hold his ground. This should create some space for me as if it has worked, I will have lost this defender. The key point now is to remember that if I am not through a gap and I want to pass, before I make that pass, I must attack the opposition's defensive line; I must straighten up, so instead of continuing to run diagonally I have to change my direction and step in towards the inside of

above. If I don't do that, the new defender who will be on me now will follow me and the ball, when I pass out he will be able to cover the intended recipient of my pass.

However, if I do threaten the inside of my defender by straightening up my running line, I stop him just enough to prevent him from drifting towards my fellow attacker. He has to cover me and protect his defensive line and if I again attack his inside shoulder as I've described I will create space for my team mate on my right. I can then make the pass to him as described in the passing chapter (left foot forward, creating a channel with my left elbow up etc.). It may be only a very small movement in towards the defence but it shows your intention and makes a huge difference in the defender's mind when he has to make a decision.

These opportunities are all created by keeping in mind the importance of attacking the defence.

Here the second defender has decided to step in and get me. I've passed to my right and my supporting team mate is away

## Exploiting the defence

Now for the key point. This is something we talk about a lot in the professional game. What we are looking at here is how to take advantage of a slow defender in the line. It could be someone that's having a bad day, someone that's slightly injured or even someone that's just out of position. Let's call this defender the 'weakest link' for now. So, how do we work the situation to our benefit?

Basically what you want to create is an isolated 2-on-1 from a 2-on-2. Agility and footwork play a huge part here. We start in a 2-on-2 with the weakest link (or mis-match) being the inside of the two defenders. Let's say I'm facing that defender. Using side steps and agility (as discussed later) I can take him on and get around him cleanly, leaving him floundering in the gap behind me. I will have run into the space he left between himself and his fellow defender, and I'm now causing the second defender to make a decision: step in and get me or stay put covering my team mate who is supporting me. Whatever the

defender decides to do, I must make sure I am always attacking the space in between – this will force him into a definite decision making it easier for me (the attacker) to read the situation. If he does decide to move across to get me, all I need to do is send out a pass to my man on the outside and he is away.

If that defender does make the tackle on me I can still create an off-load situation and pass over the top, behind me or under my arm etc. to my team mate. That's why being able to off-load is so important, as I discussed in the passing chapter. If the defender stays covering his man, there will be plenty of space in front of me to dummy and accelerate away. A win-win situation.

If I spot a mis-match or weak link in the defence on the outside then the best attacker 1 can do is to fix defender 1 then leave attacker 2 (hopefully a winger) in a 1 on 1 situation in a lot of space with defender 2 (a slow forward) who he can beat on either side with speed or footwork. Fix means to interest defenders and force them to commit to you and not your team mates.

If, however, there is a slow player in the middle of the defensive line then there is a good way

of exploiting him, by attacking the defender on the outside of the weak link and dragging him across the field fast. He will then be forced to accelerate away from the weak link who will not be able to keep up, causing a hole to appear and expand. This is when the next attacker in the line can come underneath the ball carrier on a late switch into this hole and then swerve back out again to link up with his support. Sometimes if attacking moves are executed well then it needn't even be a weak link but merely a fixed defender who is held by an attacker.

This time the defender has decided to cover my team mate and I have exploited the space that has opened up

Now picture a 4-on-4 situation. Imagine a miss pass from attacker 1 across number 2 attacker to attacker number 3. Defender 2 is held by attacker 2. Attacker 3 drags defender 3 away and attacker 4 comes underneath attacker 3 on the late switch. Defender 4 is left standing and the 4-on-4 is beaten. Any attacking move can be broken into any of the different defence-exploiting elements contained in this chapter. It is all about creating and preserving space.

Reading the switch and coming in or knowing when to stay on the outside are both very important; the decision is based on where the slow defender is in the line. These opportunities are created by footwork, anticipation and changing running lines. Understanding depth is also key in achieving both of these manoeuvres – when to hold back; when to sit flat. And of course early communication is another tool. If you tell your team mates what you are going to do they can be ready in support and vice versa.

## Practice drills

The best way to practise the various attacking options I have outlined is to do just that – practise, practise, practise. You want to get to the point where you and your team mates instinctively know what to do as situations arise on the pitch. And when there are options, remember communication is the key. If you are at full pelt and an instant decision has to be taken – yell it out. If you have practised and your team mates know what you mean by 'I can see the gap, I can see the gap,' then the move should go like clockwork. Whatever the situation, there is always a space to attack. If the space is very small and running into it means you run at the defender's arms and not directly at him,

that is a positive outcome. At least, that's the theory.

For practice drills all you need to do is set up either 2-on-1s, 2-on-2s, 3-on-3s, 4-on-4s or 3-on-2s and have the attackers running at the defenders, trying to get past them by executing a variety of moves conventionally fixing the defenders   miss passes, miss passes followed by switches, exploiting mis-matches, dummy switches etc., always bearing in mind the mantra of 'attack the defence' and 'communication'. And remember to mix the moves up so that the 'defenders' don't know what's coming and the attackers are kept on their toes.

## Agility

Understanding attacking plays and strategies, seeing and acting on the best running lines and changing angles late whilst communicating constantly with your team mates are vital to winning matches, but as I said at the outset of this chapter, the most important thing in attacking rugby is to preserve, and indeed create, space. Without space, your attack will be suffocated – nowhere to go means no penetration which means no points. Which adds up to not much fun.

The ability to create the necessary space is therefore a skill to practise and master. I've already covered aspects such as off-loading the ball in a tackle and drawing in your defender, but I haven't yet discussed creat-ing space through your own movement. This comes down to agility.

## Why is agility so important?

For me, agility is the ability to move and change your direction and speed. The ability to stay light on one's feet, with lots of little foot contacts on the toes as opposed to planting the whole foot and heel, allows the individual to react quickly; very quickly.

In defence it allows you to change direction, react to what's going on in front of you, to make tackles, and to get your feet close to the player you are trying to tackle. This means you can often make your tackles with

a big impact with your shoulder using your leg drive rather than lunging from a distance. In attack it allows you to change direction, beat opponents, and to react to other players when they have the ball. Also, in severe contact situations or when there is little time, it can be used to half beat a player, allowing you to utilise your off-loading skills to keep the ball alive. This makes the game a lot quicker and easier to play as it makes it difficult to set defensive lines. It also allows you to react to different passes that are too short, too high, or too wide – you can get to them and make the catch. Agility also works as a safety mechanism. You need it so that your body can react quickly enough to get you out of trouble, out of dangerous situations, therefore reducing the likelihood of injury.

If you enjoy the game – *really* enjoy it – but sometimes it gets a bit much for you, then when it gets a bit much, just don't do it.

## Side steps and spins

In terms of attacking, perhaps the most important – and certainly one of the most satisfying – aspects of agility is the ability to side step and beat an opponent. He's left staring at thin air and you are away into the space.

There are two different types of side steps to consider when we have the ball and are trying to beat a player: one-footed and two-footed side steps. There is also the spin move, which is really just a further development of the two-footed side step.

The one-footed side step is a pure one direction change. The deception is created by both the change of direction and the change of pace but in essence the change of direction *at* pace. A player runs to one side before stepping back off the outside foot to go back the other way. This means that the left foot

pushes to the right or the right foot pushes to the left. It's important that the outside foot does the step, and that the pace is maintained or even accelerated with the change of direction.

The one-footed side step is most favoured by wingers or outer backs such as full backs and outside centres. Imagine the scene: a player might be running for the corner on the outside with an opposition full back coming across to make the tackle and prevent a try. Then, at the last moment, the attacking player suddenly steps back inside the covering defender, off the outside foot, and he is under the posts.

Try to free up the inside arm to perform a hand-off by moving the ball to the outer arm away from the defender you have just evaded.

HOW TO PLAY RUGBY MY WAY

## Top tip

Deceive an opponent by using a one-footed or two-footed side step or even a spin and then, once past the tackle, learn how to off-load the ball one-handed, using the other hand to fend off the defender. This is great for getting behind and breaking strong defensive lines. It is important that a support player stays close and follows you through the line.

The other type of side step is a two-footed step, more often used by inside backs like myself or players like Jason Robinson. This is where your two feet land on the ground almost at the same time and the direction change is then created by pushing off the outside foot (which should be the last to hit the ground) with help from the inside foot. You make the decision as to which direction you are going in very late, often right at the last second, therefore making this step difficult to defend against. Both feet actually leave the floor and it's very difficult to know the order in which the feet are going to land back down and which direction the player will run. Using the head as a tool for deception is also very helpful here, as you can look or fake towards the opposite direction that you intend to travel. It's not performed with as much pace as the one-footed side step because of the lack of space available to build up speed. Sometimes it has to be done from almost standing still, or just moving forward. It is then vital you use short fast steps to accelerate away. Without this the step is rendered ineffective because the lack of speed allows the deceived defender to regain his ground.

The two-footed side step is more commonly used by the inside backs, 9s, 10s or 12s for example, where the space available to work on a change of direction is tight and you need to make the decision late. This double step also leads into another form of agility and movement, which is the spin.

## The Spin

The two-footed side step in a tight confined area can be extended to perform a very useful evasive move in contact situations: a spin move. It is fairly simple and is centred around two changes from the two-footed step. It is still vital that the push comes from the outside foot – the last to hit the ground. The first change is that the other foot does not help to push away but remains where it is and acts as a pivot rotating through 180 degrees. The second point is that the head turns quickly through 180 degrees which leads the body into the spin and makes the manoeuvre tight and effective. A two-footed side step that pushes left off the right foot will become a clockwise spin and push off the left foot for an anti-clockwise spin. The spin is a fantastic tool for evading big tackles and getting out of trouble. It can also free up the hands for a vital offload. Practise and do not be afraid to use it.

## Avoiding tackles

The ability to swerve, change direction and fool an opponent isn't just important for creating space in open play. The reality is that sometimes you get caught, or almost caught. You might be right up against the defensive line and a one-footed or even a two-footed side step will be impossible because a defender is bearing down on top of you.

In that circumstance, the best way to avoid the big hit is mostly to make a small change of direction at the last minute – and agility comes in very handy for this. If you are up on your toes, with light, fast foot work, when you see a potential tackle coming at you, you should be able to immediately rely on your ability to spin out of the tackle or move out of the way. Even if you take a short pass and you look up and a defender's right there, just the split second to swerve slightly and take the tackle on your outer leg rather than your full chest is often important to avoid getting put down and having no chance of keeping the ball alive.

One of the most important and underperformed skills is changing direction and side stepping before you receive the ball, allowing you to create the space and extra time you need to play in the face of the opposition and deceive defenders. All this, even before you have the ball in your hands.

## Practice drills

For agility, as indeed for all practice sessions, do it in manageable bits. And keep it varied. For instance, for a warm-up use cones and weave through them to practise side steps, say repeating five times; then do three sets of drills with a ball (passing or handling); then shadow a team mate who is practising side steps and footwork (shadowing is great to sharpen your reactions and anticipation of how an opponent might move); and finally try ten sets of you as the attacker trying to side step the 'defender' in a small restricted area with a try line to attack at one end. That's a perfect routine. What you've covered is ball handling, and using your footwork, then beating a man. You've got your brain focusing on your skills in the warm-up and it will only have taken 20 minutes or so, leaving you time to focus on other skills such as kicking or tackling. Suddenly, within an hour, you've covered all the basics.

Here is a specific exercise to work on agility. The aim of this exercise is to try and ensure that the movements become second nature, meaning that you can perform them under severe pressure when there is very little time to think.

One player stands in the middle and is surrounded by two or more players. One outside player throws a ball to the player in the middle, who catches it. The ball doesn't have to be a rugby ball – it can be a tennis ball, a sponge ball, or any other type. On catching the ball, the middle player side steps or turns or spins and then off-loads it either back to the original player who threw it, or to another player standing around the circle. The aim is

to perform this very quickly in short, sharp bursts. Maybe take turns for 20 seconds each in the middle catching and passing and moving as many times as possible.

The next progressive stage for this exercise is to then place another person in the middle. This second person's task is to crowd the player trying to receive the ball. On getting the ball, the receiver has to try and get away from the blocking player, creating space, before he off-loads the ball.

Learn how to off-load the ball with one hand, two hands, behind the back, over the head, and in any number of different ways.

**Playing other sports like football and basketball are brilliant for helping the body learn new moves and making them feel natural**

## Blackie's secret

Jonny's agility drills are born out of soccer work. Soccer players generally have better feet than rugby players. Jonny's regime was, very much at first, based on Kevin Keegan. Kevin was fantastic at chopping and changing directions and altering his pace. He was very difficult to mark as a footballer. I would get Jonny to mimic a lot of Kevin's movement, without Jonny really knowing that Kevin was the source of what we did. He would copy the movements, and he would create space ahead of him. You need to be able to give yourself just a split second, just a little gap, to exploit.

## Best in the business

Jonathan Davies of Wales. His understanding of running lines and his anticipation of what attackers and defenders were going to do or were trying to do was immense, especially when he played rugby league as a centre or full back.

**Skills**

# Kicking

## The basics

# Kicking
## The basics

There are many different kicks in rugby – on the move, stationary, kicking from a tee, defenders rushing at you, looking for height, looking for distance, searching for position. Every kick is different, because every game is different.

I'll be dealing with the individual kicks in the following chapters, but there are very important points that they all have in common. These are the core techniques that must become second nature to you. The same applies in passing and tackling – you have to get the basics right before you can develop, refine and expand your repertoire. If you haven't mastered the fundamentals, then when you are in the thick of things in a game, under pressure and with little time, you try something new, you run the risk of it all unravelling – at crucial moments.

So that is what this introductory chapter is all about – the common denominators that link all types of kicks. Some specialist kicks may require that you tweak the points I will outline here (and I will cover those in the coming chapters) but fundamentally, if you become strong in these elements you will be properly equipped when you run out on the field of play.

### The J-shape© swing
*Kicking coach Dave Alred's special invention*

You will see that I refer to this over and over again in the coming chapters. It is the key building block for all kicking. That's why Dave Alred talks to me about it all the time and why we are dealing with it right here at the beginning. It is that important.

Kicking is about putting power through the sweet spot of the ball in the direction you want the ball to travel. Regardless of the type of kick, and regardless of what may be going on around you, you must feel in total control and not like it's hit and miss whether you are successful or not. The J-shape© swing will give you that confidence.

The J-shape© swing allows you to totally dominate the three-dimensional aspects of the kick – you will be in control of the height, distance, and direction. This is because the swing connects and sends power through the

HOW TO PLAY RUGBY MY WAY

# Reaching your potential is the key.

middle of the ball in the direction the ball needs to travel. The J-shape© swing also enables you to use your entire body to create power and force, therefore delivering explosive energy with less effort. This means you can be more controlled, more deliberate, and the ball has a greater chance of going where it needs to go.

It is called a J-shape© swing because the initial part of the swing, when you pull your leg back, is the rounded part of the 'J', and the rest of the swing represents the leg travelling up to the top of the 'J', i.e. a dead straight line. Depending on which foot you are kicking with, the 'J' may look backwards, i.e. 'Ⴐ' as in

the series of photographs above, but the principle is exactly the same. This straight line is very important as it means that when your foot connects with the ball it will stay in contact with it for a long time, always in the direction you want it to go. You are therefore transferring more power from leg and body to ball that way.

The other type of swing you see people perform is known as a C-shape©, which is what we're trying to avoid. In that swing the foot makes contact with the ball on the rounded part of the 'C' (the 'C' might look backwards if you are kicking with your right foot but the principle is the same), and continues in a curve.

As a result, the foot stays in contact with the ball for a very short period. Your leg will not be transferring power through the ball in the direction the ball needs to go, but will instead be channelling it in the wrong direction. In addition, all your weight will follow your leg which means you are wasting energy.

## Weight shift

Another factor of the J-shape© swing is the shift in body weight. That's why we talk about the non-kicking foot moving towards the target. Yes, the non-kicking foot is firmly planted on the ground for balance when you actually make contact with the ball, but your

body should be moving forward, creating momentum that sends the ball in the correct direction. So with place kicking we talk about pushing from the tee towards the posts. With drop goals and punts it is the same principle. For those kicks we talk about finishing on our toes, not the heels of our feet, because even if it's tiny, the fact that your body moves to your toes makes it much more effective than if you finish back on your heels. This idea of weight transfer is why it is so important to master the drop punt on the run, because when you execute that particular kick correctly your body weight naturally follows, making for a very accurate and powerful kick.

## Posture

The other key element of kicking is having a strong posture, which enables you to create maximum force through the ball and perform the J-shape© swing without risking injury. Strong posture (above left) is about being upright, strong through the hips and the core of your body so there's no collapsing to one side or the other, enabling you to maintain a firm base for the leg to swing through, connect with the ball, and stay straight and tall. A weak posture (above right) means that your weight is over to one side and your leg has to swing in the opposite direction to compensate and balance, reducing power. Swinging your leg in a straight path is far more effective and eco-nomical – you don't have to try so hard and therefore you reduce the possibility of pulled muscles or other injuries.

### Hand on foot posture exercise

This exercise allows you to understand correct posture. Sit in a chair and be aware of your posture – body upright and strong through the hips and the abdominal area, the sternum pushed up, the chest set tall. Have someone push on the top of your foot so that your leg is bent. Remain in the chair and now push against the hand, keeping your posture and your leg straight. Feel your quad muscle (the dominant

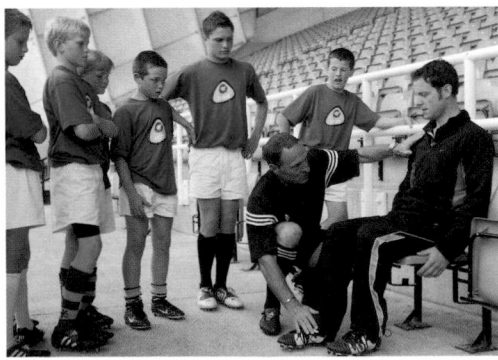

## Alred's expertise

*The pane of glass*

It is vital that you understand the idea of a J-shape© leg swing, I use an example of breaking a pane of glass. Imagine the plane of glass cutting you in half between the eyes and right through the length of your body. When you punt you should ensure that your foot stays on the same side of the glass. One of the practices resembles a silly walk. For a left-footed kick you swing the left leg up and through and keep your right arm straight out in front, which will help in keeping the right shoulder forward, which stops your foot rotating offline when you kick. This is important for all types of kick. Your leg and arms should not cross, staying parallel to each other. This will also ensure at the end of the kick that your chest is correctly positioned – facing directly at the target. For a right-footed kick, you have your left arm out straight in front. You should be imagining that your arm is holding one side of the pane of glass and your foot stays the other side. If they cross the glass will break, and your foot would have swung in a C-shape©, which means there would be a chance of a miss hit, and wasted power.

muscle in the front of your thigh) doing the work and transferring power through to the resisting hand using the top of the foot. If you lose your posture, collapsing to one side or try to push against the hand you will find you are not able to use the top of the foot and you bring your inside leg muscles into play – and they are nowhere near as powerful as the quads. This is the same in goal kicking. If you have the correct posture you can tilt your foot, making it hard, and use your quad muscle to kick with. If you're in a weak posture, you will find you use the inside of your foot to kick and the inside leg muscle, transferring half the power to the ball, with greater risk of slicing or hooking it.

Just think about how people kick instinctively. If a group of people are each asked to kick a football as high above them as they can, how many would stand there, lean over to their side and try to kick it with their instep? Not many I suspect. Far more would just stand there and really try and thump the ball straight up with the top of their foot. The reason people kick like that is because it allows you to use the strongest muscle, the strongest part of your foot, and the stronger posture.

## Head position

If you notice, on a good leg swing, when you see the finishing position of a goal kick or a punt, the head, which is the heaviest part of the body and therefore determines the balance, remains directly above the navel, the centre of gravity (top right). So you finish in a dead line, ensuring that the J-shape© swing is intact. However, if your head is off your centre of gravity and over the outside of your kicking leg, it causes you to lean away into a weak position, removing your power and accuracy so you have to correct yourself by swinging round the dreaded C-shape© swing (bottom right).

## Aim

Visualise aiming for a specific tiny black dot. You want to feel the confidence of being in total control of the ball – and being as specific as possible as to where the ball will be going is part of building that confidence. It's a bit like a golfer approaching a green. Rather than aiming generally for the green, he or she will pinpoint a specific mark on the upper edge of the green, or wherever is appropriate – perhaps the hole itself. In rugby the equivalent is aiming for a black dot on a single post or a seat number in the crowd. If you can aim for a specific point and then hit it, that's absolutely fantastic; but there is room for

error – If you miss by a small amount, or even by a reasonable amount, when you are kicking from anywhere in front of the posts the ball still goes over. Everyone cheers in the crowd, and you can run back thinking, 'That wasn't my best kick, but you know, it was three points.' That will do me.

HOW TO PLAY RUGBY MY WAY

## Practice drills

For all types of kicking, don't just mechanically do repetitions for the sake of them. Try and focus in short spurts. When punting, try five kicks on your left, five on your right, another five on your left, and finish with five on your right. By doing that you give yourself a closed boundary around the skills and you can concentrate on getting each kick spot on. If you just continue to shoot away, you end up with good kicks, bad kicks, a great kick, an awful kick, three average kicks, three good ones and a bad one. If that happens, it is easy to lose focus on what made the great one great and the bad ones bad. That doesn't help. It is much better to do numbered sets of kicks with real focus.

It is also important to mix it up. Often when I kick, I might do a restart, a kick to touch, a couple of spiral bombs, a couple of drop goals, two goal kicks, two more restarts, then

## Alred's expertise

In the manic pressure of a game situation, no strike on the ball will ever be perfect because you cannot guarantee exactly how you will receive the pass, which way your body will be facing, what the opposition is doing and where the wind is blowing. It is important to be able to execute a good enough kick in as short a time as possible when you are under pressure. It's a good idea to have one or two simple cues to help you to do that. For me, I think of focussing on the middle of the ball and try to connect there with the bones in the top of my foot. That normally gets enough power through the ball in the direction I want it to travel to get me out of trouble. Some players feel secure placing their hand under the middle of the ball when they drop it, and hitting the point on the ball where their hand was. Another cue you might want to think about is hitting up towards the target as you connect with the ball, making sure you finish on your toes, this also helps to get your weight forward. Keeping your opposite shoulder forward helps you to shift your weight in the direction the ball is travelling.

six punts. Mixing it up helps you to simulate playing conditions. Now that doesn't mean that it's not good to practise a lot of goal kicks – but I always make sure to do that early in a training week. As match day approaches, I switch my training pattern to ensure I am confident with performing in the wide variety of kicks I will encounter during the game. That can make all the difference when executing kicks under pressure.

# Punting

# Punting

**P**unting is the art of kicking the ball from hand before it hits the floor. It's used a great deal in rugby for gaining field position, relieving pressure, up-and-unders, cross kicks and grubber kicks. The most important point is to understand that punting is a skill performed with the entire body, not just the leg. Body position is hugely important to ensure your weight shift transfers power in the direction you want the ball to travel.

There are two types of drop punts. One is when the player remains stationary after the kick, and the other is a running drop punt, where a player continues to run forward after kicking. The initial steps for both skills are the same, but the difference occurs after the ball has been struck. In this chapter we will also be covering the spiral and grubber kick, variations on the punt.

## How to do it – the basics

The ball is held in a vertical position, with the seams pointing forward to the target and the fingers spread, holding the ball. You use the right hand on the right-hand side of the ball to drop onto the right foot, and the left hand on the left-hand side of the ball to drop it onto the left foot. The other hand in each case helps to guide the ball down. The kick is performed by connecting with and pushing the bottom third of the ball forward with the top of your foot creating a back spinning motion in the direction you want the ball to travel.

For the kick itself, it's important to have a hard foot, point the toe downward and make sure the punt comes directly off the centre of the top part of your boot, the hardest part of the foot with the most area to connect. I have a piece of rubber put on the top part of my boot for extra strength. If you perform the kick correctly you should feel yourself making a sweet strike on the ball. This feeling can be increased by pointing the toes of the kicking foot, thus dominating the impact with the ball and making it ping off the kicking foot.

The contact on the foot should not only feel hard and deliberate, but also very very comfortable. The sound of the contact should be a real thud, as opposed to a clap of the hands, or a slapping sound. This sound illustrates that your foot is dominating the contact, and your body weight has travelled through the sweet spot of the ball in the direction it needs to go.

A hugely important coaching point is to think of keeping the opposite shoulder to the kicking leg forwards. This stops the shoulder pulling back and causing a rotation in the leg swing, a C-shape©! It helps the weight shift travel forwards and keeps your chest pointing to the target, ensuring no wasted energy. If a ball is struck well the chest position will be a good indicator of whether the technique was in place.

It's also important, in both the drop punt and the running drop punt, that you drop the ball over your kicking leg, not in front of your crutch. Otherwise your leg will have to come from the outside inwards in order to collect the ball, pulling or slicing your kick depending on the contact – the dreaded C-swing I mentioned in the introduction. For a right-footed kick, if the ball is dropped in front of the crutch, the ball will travel left if hit well, and for a left-footed kick it will travel right if not dropped correctly. If the ball is placed too far out over the kicking leg, too wide, then the outside of the foot will connect with the inner panel of the ball and will cause a sliced kick. However, if the ball is held out over the leg,

HOW TO PLAY RUGBY MY WAY

then the foot can make contact dead in line, and send the ball in a straight arc to the target. A good way to think of this is to put the ball on the end of the swing, and not use the swing to find the ball.

The leg should make contact with the ball in the J-shape© swing. When the ball is kicked through the sweet spot to the target, your weight and power are taken through and

upwards as the leg itself comes through and upwards. Utilising body and leg means more power, less effort, more accuracy and control, and fewer injuries; all positives.

### Avoiding injuries

Kicking with your body and not just your leg helps to avoid strains and injuries. If you kick with just your leg you put a lot of force through your pelvic joint, your groin, your hip joints, and through your back. Everything's put under a lot of strain because there's a lot of leg swing and nothing to control it. So instead of using your leg for the power, use your leg and your body together. When your foot strikes the ball, your leg swings through and your body goes with it, giving it that extra force and making it feel more comfortable. You don't need to kick it as hard to get it as far and because you are not trying too hard you can improve accuracy, and be more in control. Here the hard foot adds enormous benefit. I think 'Kick it sweeter, not harder' is a helpful phrase to remind yourself to point the toe.

## How to do it – running drop punts

The running drop punt is used as a cross kick. This could perhaps be to a winger on the far side of the pitch, or even a hard low kick into the corner because the ball can sometimes backspin where it lands on the floor and sit in the corner. This puts pressure on the opposition and can create attacking opportunities. There are a few key points for executing a solid running drop punt.

Placement of the hand on the ball is very important. For a left-footed kick, hold the ball on the side with your left hand, fingers spread, and make sure your hand stays in contact with the ball as it begins to drop. What you must avoid is holding the ball on the top and pushing it onto the foot. Your hand is there to balance and guide the ball – nothing more. Hit up to the top of the target as for a normal drop punt.

When kicking a running drop punt, it is important, once the kick has been executed, for your next step to be with your kicking foot, i.e. if you kick with your right foot you should land on your right foot and then run through towards the target. This creates a backspin on the ball where the ball spins directly backwards towards you because you are pushing the bottom third forward and it travels straight to the target. Running through the ball ensures that your all-important body weight travels from the point of contact through the ball and towards the target, thus taking the pressure off the leg and creating more power with less effort. It also creates a straight kicking line. Your chest should finish facing the target.

There are several pointers that can be used to assess whether your kick has been performed well. Did your chest remain pointed towards the target? Did the kick feel comfortable? Did you have a hard foot? Was the sound of the kick correct? Did the ball spin? And obviously the end result of where the ball goes is important.

## Practice drill

A good drill to practise is simply to run and kick to each other, say 10, 15 yards apart, with both feet. After a while you will be able to build this up to execute longer kicks.

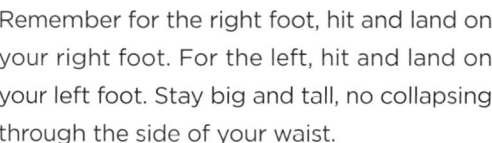

Remember for the right foot, hit and land on your right foot. For the left, hit and land on your left foot. Stay big and tall, no collapsing through the side of your waist.

Maybe then get your partner to run in any direction and try to land a running drop punt in his path so he doesn't have to break stride to catch it. Also work with a winger and land a set of running drop punts in the try area for him to run onto and score. You can also aim for the ball to land and stop rolling as close to a corner flag as possible. This can be made into a competition with some of your friends but always ensure you use both feet.

HOW TO PLAY RUGBY MY WAY

## How to do it – drop punts

The drop punt is used in many different situations because it is versatile, accurate and easy to catch. If I want to disguise a kick across to my winger, I can hit it on the run, low and hard, and he has a good chance of catching it. As with running drop punts, I can kick it to corners, and because of the backspin the ball might sit nicely in the corner, forcing the opposition to kick it out. I would use the stationary drop punt to kick to touch from very narrow angles when I need to be very accurate. I also use it for big high up-and-unders if I want to chase and catch.

The technique is exactly the same as for the running drop punt, but this time it's important that you finish on your toes. This ensures that your weight is still going forward through the ball, since it is not possible to create the weight transfer by the mere fact that you will already be running (i.e. you will be almost stationary for drop punts). In addition, your non-kicking foot must move forward after the kick. The fact that

you are not running forward when you execute the kick also means that it is very important to stop your body from rotating and kicking around the ball in the C-shape©. You must concentrate on the J-shape© swing in which the foot connects and then follows the ball, sending it in the direction it needs to go. The difficulty is that your body can often be pulled around in a C-shape© because of your opposite shoulder pulling back – for a right-footed kick that would be the left shoulder, and vice versa for a left-footed kick. If this happens you will end up directing the ball away from where it should be travelling. This is why it's important, along with staying on the toes, to keep your opposite shoulder forward so that the chest remains pointed at the ball. Remember Dave Alred's 'pane of glass' technique that he explained on page 131.

So visualise a kick off your right foot. The ball will be out over the right leg, and you will be keeping your left side forward which allows you to swing your leg in a comfortable back and forth motion under your body.

## Pitfalls

**Kicking across the ball with a C-shape© leg swing that wastes energy and breeds a hit-and-miss inconsistency.**

Remember, if your left side falls back on a right-footed kick, it pulls your leg with you in a C-shape© and you will hook the ball, or have to use the muscles of your inner thigh rather than your quad muscle to kick it straight – losing power and accuracy. If your left side stays forward, or you think of having your chest directed towards the ball, then this will enable you to make the kick and continue to move forward in the line the ball needs to travel. In addition, if you have your left shoulder back you will lean back and be in a weak position. All three elements combined will mean that your kick will be nowhere near as powerful as it should have been.

After the kick you should have a balanced finish. By that I mean that after you hit the drop punt, you should be able to stay balanced on your non-kicking leg with very little effort. You shouldn't be tilted back on that leg struggling to stay up or in a weak collapsing position.

Another key point in kicking drop punts is to make sure you create a 'gate' with your two hands so that your leg kicks through that gate. So, with a left-footed kick, both hands initially support the ball, then the right hand drops off to the right side, parallel to the ball, creating a gap between the right hand and the ball. This is the gate, and as you go to kick you should be visualising kicking through that gate.

In terms of distance and height, remember that the kick itself is a three-dimensional kick. You have total control of the height, distance, power and direction. So, if you want height, you simply swing higher and connect with the ball slightly higher up from the ground. For a lower kick, you should let the ball drop lower, your body should be tilted forward and the swing is longer and lower. Sometimes tilting the ball slightly forward can help here too. However, you must still connect just behind the point of the ball and push the bottom third up. The leg swing is always in the direction the ball needs to travel, with your opposite shoulder forward and always finishing on your toes.

**Visualise kicking through the gap created between your right hand (for a left-footed kick) and the ball**

# I'm someone who doesn't want to let anyone down.

## How to do it - spirals

We use the spiral because the ball travels further and quicker than a regular punt and therefore it can be very effective in certain circumstances. For instance, if I have a bit of space in the corner of the pitch and plan on kicking, but then see the opposition full back coming across, I will want to beat him to the corner. In that situation a spiral will be ideal because it will get there a lot quicker than a drop punt. Also, when a spiral hits the floor, it can skid and roll on very quickly. Defensive full backs and wingers hate that. There is a specialist kick called a spiral bomb which you would never use if your intention is to chase and regain the

ball. The spiral bomb is hit very high and comes down at pace and weaving all over the place. It is ideal to use to put the opposition full back under a lot of pressure because he can lose the ball in flight and not make his catch – that's just the kind of disorganisation you want to create, a loose ball close to the try line or a knock-on at the very least.

The standing drop punt and the spiral kick are exactly the same kick, apart from two changes. One is the positioning of the ball on the drop and the second is the slight off-setting of the body. These two parts fit together and it's done by a reference to a clock face.

For a right-footed kick, your body starts facing 12 o'clock, with the ball in front, and held pointing forward with one hand either side. Then, turn your body so that you are facing 1 o'clock and turn the the left tip of the ball so that it is pointing to 11 o'clock. Now the 12 o'clock line goes through the middle of the ball and the middle of your chest. This opens up the sweet spot, which is exactly the same shape as the entire ball, just smaller and in the very middle of the ball. I discussed this idea of a gate to kick through in the section on drop punts. Here that gate still

## Alred's expertise

**If you want to try and destroy the opposition fullback, send them a spiral bomb to deal with. The basics are the same as for all spiral punting but the foot makes contact with the ball a lot higher off the ground. You should think of making contact with the ball above your waist and with the ball placed with the nose pointing up by about 30 degrees. Keep your opposite shoulder forward and ensure you finish on your toes.**

applies but there is an additional element – the ball is presented as if it had been placed gently on a shelf. By this I mean your hands are placed under the ball, towards either end, supporting it like a shelf, but the gate is still there to kick through.

To perform the kick, the ball is placed over the kicking leg and the top of your foot connects with the dead centre of the sweet spot, and you kick through the ball, in exactly the same

# No matter how painful, how much there is to lose, how difficult it may seem or how impossible the situation on the field, it's important to still attack with a totally positive mental outlook. Never give in.

The common misconception is that the leg swing is needed to impart spin on the ball, which is why people kick in a C-shape© and try to make the ball spin themselves. This wastes a lot of power and creates a huge margin for error since there is very little time when the foot is in contact with the ball. As I have described previously, with a J-shape© swing, the foot is in contact a lot longer, and throughout all that time it is sending the ball in the direction it needs to go. The J-shape© swing uses the hard top of the foot while the C-shape© swing uses the outside of the boot. This is a good example of why many poor kicks executed with a J-shape© swing will turn out to be absolutely fine.

For a left-footed spiral kick, everything's reversed. So from a 12 o'clock start with the ball in front of you, you turn to 11 o'clock and the right tip of the ball points towards 1 o'clock, again opening up the central sweet spot. When the ball is placed over the leg, the top of your left foot can hit hard through the middle of the ball towards 11 o'clock, and with your hip joint bring your leg and chest round to 12. Again all the checklists apply – the sound of the kick, the spin, chest to the target on finish, weight on your toes, the direction of the ball. And as with punts, the spiral kick is a three-dimensional kick meaning you are in total charge of all elements – distance, accuracy and height.

**Present the ball as if it was being placed gently on a shelf**

way as drop punting, the left side of your body and your left shoulder always pushed forward for a right-footed kick. The body and leg swing is directed towards one o'clock but the natural ball-and-socket joint movement of the hip will bring the leg round to 12 o'clock. This also imparts the spin on the ball, allowing the ball to be kicked with a thud and the spiral to take place as it travels towards the target. This is a J-shape© swing. You need to get your power through the ball so hit up to the top of the target and finish on your toes, which is exactly the same as a drop punt.

Again, when punting low, lean forwards a bit, let the ball drop a little lower and maybe tilt the front nose of the ball towards the ground slightly.

The spiral kick can be performed on the run as in the running drop punt, and all the same points discussed in that section apply equally here, e.g. landing on the kicking foot, etc. The one thing you have to remember here, of course, is that your run into the ball is from an offset position, and that the 1 o'clock, 11 o'clock rules still apply to both feet, as does the ball and socket hip joint swing.

The kicks can be performed in different ways. Low kicks, for example, are performed in the same manner as a drop punt, with the body tilted forward and the ball dropped low to the ground. The medium height kicks are performed as I've described, and are great for touch kicks – both in open play and off penalties and free kicks. The high kick is when the ball is held a greater distance off the floor and the foot comes up to connect with that and for a spiral bomb, the ball is held even higher

and the foot comes into contact a lot further off the ground.

## Grubber kicks

These are very useful kicks and are used to create scoring opportunities in the opposition's try area – when there is no fullback covering you can pop one through for your team mates to chase and hopefully score. Rugby balls are notoriously unpredictable in the way they bounce – which means a kick through and a chase can still be a bit of a lottery as to whether your team can get your hands on the ball or not. Grubber kicks increase the odds in your favour because they move end-over-end and therefore it is easier to predict where the ball will go. And even if the defence does get to the ball first, because grubber kicks travel along the ground the defender will have to stoop down to pick the ball up – giving your attackers a couple more seconds to get there, and bundle him into touch or over the try line. They can also be used to create good attacking positions when the kick is pushed towards the corner, forcing

Kicking the top end
of the ball is the key
difference in
grubber kicks and
you achieve that by
dropping the ball in
a horizontal position
to the ground. But
remember to
remain flexible in
undertaking
grubber kicks

the opposition to kick into touch, and thereby winning a lineout in a dangerous position.

Grubber kicks are exactly the same as drop punts, except that you kick the top end of the ball as opposed to the bottom end of the ball. The ball is dropped horizontal to the ground facing forwards rather than perpendicular to the ground. The ball is struck a little closer to the ground too. But everything else applies, especially finishing on your toes and running through the ball in the direction you want it to travel.

It is important to be able to adapt with grubber kicks because often it might not be possible to face head on or run through the ball so what helps is to think of pushing your leg to the target and getting a strong solid feeling from the contact which should be with a hard foot. It may be useful to practise using your instep or even the outside of your foot, but the same principles apply.

## Practice drills

It is essential to spend a lot of time on your punting skills. You need to be confident in all the fundamentals because in a game situation, from a pass, there are very few perfect kicks. This is because the ball can arrive in your hands in an awkward way and it can be hard to get it in the fraction of a second you might have, on to the foot and exactly where it needs to be. However, if the majority of the key points are in place, for example the hard foot, the ball out over the leg, the left side (for a right-footed kick) forward and the top of the foot connecting more or less with the sweet spot of the ball – then the kick should feel good enough and it should get the job done.

Under pressure, the body tends to speed up, and when the body speeds up it reverts to a C-shape© swing. In order to counteract that possibility of a big slice or hook, you again need to be on top of these basic points – make sure they are ingrained before you work

# I try to set the good example that if I ever perform anything, I give it everything I possibly can.

## Best in the Business

Paul Grayson. Paul always has had a great feel for the ball and is probably the most consistent ball striker I have ever played or practised with.

off actual passes. Once the foundations are in place, and you begin to run drills where the ball is passed to you, this is obviously a very game-realistic scenario. It also helps getting someone to run at you with a tackle shield held above their head, trying to charge down your kick. This adds to the realism of the practice and skills can therefore only improve.

Remember always, however, to do the basics first. For me, in a week's training before a game, I spend Monday, Tuesday, Wednesday going over and practising the foundations of the skill. Really making sure that I'm happy and comfortable with the way I'm performing before moving onto kicking from a pass and putting myself under pressure on about Thursday and Friday. This allows me, as the match draws nearer, to get more realistic practice in.

# Place kicking

# Place kicking

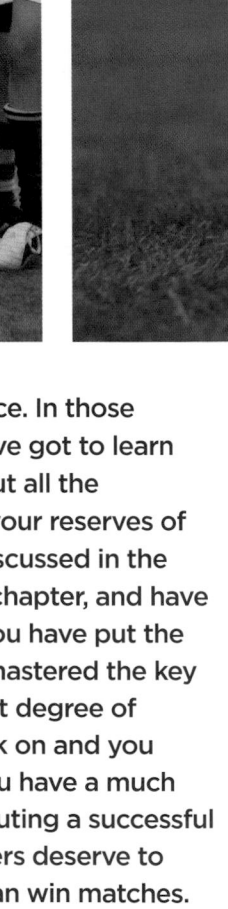

**P**lace kicking is one of the most nerve-racking and potentially rewarding of all the skills in this book. Resting on the shoulders – or more accurately in the boot – of the goal kicker can be two points if it is a conversion after a try, or three points for a penalty. It is called place kicking because that is exactly what you do – you place the ball on the ground for the sole purpose of taking a kick. In fact, nowadays almost everyone places the ball on a kicking tee but it used to be that you would either use a small mound of sand or even just grub up the grass to create your tee. Whatever you do, the principle is the same – your ball is teed up and you are going to kick for goal.

Because this is the only one of the skills in this book that you perform purely on an individual dead-ball basis – that's where the nerves can come in. You might be facing boos, whistles or it might be the last kick of the game with

the result in the balance. In those circumstances you have got to learn how to focus, block out all the distractions, tap into your reserves of mental toughness I discussed in the Practice and training chapter, and have the knowledge that you have put the practice in and have mastered the key basics. If you have that degree of confidence to fall back on and you know your routine, you have a much better chance of executing a successful kick – good goal kickers deserve to kick their goals and can win matches.

## How to do it

### Ball placement

Setting the ball up correctly is the first step. For younger players, using a higher tee makes it easier to kick, and it's a lot lighter on the groin and leg muscles. So the higher the tee the better at a young age; as you get older and get more used to kicking, you can decide what sort of tee suits your style best. A lot of the principles of punting apply to place kicking, except instead of the leg swing operating through the channel of back and forth under the body, here the swing takes place through a sideways plane using your upper quad muscle again.

Set the ball up on the tee slightly forward, and if the ball has a valve in the seam, always try to have that pointing forward. Always have the seam pointing to the target wherever you're aiming – so to aim in front of me, I place the seam dead straight, right through the middle of the posts. I also like to have the ball tilted away from me, leaning right for a right-footed kick and left for a left-footed kick. This helps to open up the ball's sweet spot.

# Make sure you are kicking with a hard foot to help maximise the output of power through the ball. You are looking for a 'ping' off the foot rather than a slap.

### Technique

The ball is kicked using a hard foot with a pointed toe – you want to really nail the ball on your foot. Contact should be made just between your big toe knuckle and the bone at the top of your foot, right over your instep. Your mentality should be, 'I'm going to send this ball exactly where I want it to go.' Dominate the ball, do not let it dominate you.

As with all the kicks we have been discussing, the key point is to make sure you transfer the power of your body and leg through the ball and in the direction you want it to travel. What you are looking to achieve is to get the amount of energy coming out of the kick to be very close to the amount you put in. This is accomplished by making sure your foot stays along the line you want the ball to travel, sending it exactly where it needs to go. Once again you must avoid energy wasted on a C-shape© swing round the corner. Making sure you are kicking with a hard foot also helps maximise this output of power through the ball. You are looking for a 'ping' off the foot rather than a slap. Unlike in drop punting, your approach to the ball in place kicking is from roughly a 45 degree angle, rather than straight on. So in your set up, take three or four steps back, in line with the ball and the posts, and then for a right-footed kicker, take two, three or four steps to the left; or two, three or four steps to the right for a left-footed kicker. Otherwise all the key principles from punting still apply, e.g. chest pointing to the ball in a strong position, hit up and get your weight to shift through the ball towards the target.

Where your foot connects with the ball is critical. If you hit the sweet spot, you will be transferring maximum power and energy through the ball. And remember, place kicks are three-dimensional kicks – there's no point in me kicking along the bottom of the ball with my foot low to the ground because I need to send the ball to its target and therefore need to determine the height. So you need to visualise the exact point of impact – just on the inside of the panel next to the seam that you have lined up with the middle of the posts, about a third of the way up the ball. This allows your foot to connect with and go through the middle of the sweet spot, and then continue forwards, coming out two-thirds of the way up

## Pitfalls

**Kicking with a C-shape® swing which wastes energy and introduces the possibility of more errors in your technique. Also not pointing your toe to create a hard foot and not finishing forwards in the direction the ball needs to travel.**

through the ball, sending it travelling in a direct line.

Once you have connected with the ball it is important that you create that weight transfer through the ball, so your chest goes to the

## Alred's expertise

Be very specific in your focus of exactly where you are aiming. Take dead aim and focus on the smallest possible target you can imagine. Sometimes we aim for an imaginary woman called 'Doris' who sits in a specific seat behind the goalposts holding a newspaper. We don't just aim at her, we aim for the newspaper. We may even aim for a particular article on the front page. If you can regularly come close to this target, then kicking from anywhere on the field should not worry you.

target, and you kick with your entire body. It's more comfortable, it's less stress on the groin, the ball travels in a straight line, the contact is sweet and altogether it should be very effective and feel great.

So to sum up: 45 degrees set up, chest pointing to the ball as you make the kick, focusing on the inside of that panel, connect with a hard foot, and send the ball along an imaginary wire to its target, then land on the same leg.

### Strong body position

A strong position in goal kicking is: the non-kicking foot alongside the ball, chest pointing to the ball, the tee in line with your crutch, kicking foot behind the ball, and the hard part of the foot lined up, ready to strike the ball one-third of the way up. That position is what gives you all the power.

Having connected and swung up through the ball, the next thing to look at is having a balanced finish. It is important you finish forward to ensure that your body moves towards the target after impact. You must concentrate on keeping your opposite shoulder forward as you make the kick. I covered this in the introduction to kicking but it is worth reiterating. For a left-foot kick, your right shoulder should be forward – don't be bent at the waist with your shoulder twisting to the left or downwards or back; it should just be forward. If your shoulder is allowed to go back, you lose the strong position, the bigness through your chest and the core of your body, and you will start pulling your leg through a C-shape© follow through. This means your weight will have been pulled around and you won't have channelled all your energy correctly in the direction the ball needs to be travelling.

However, with your shoulder position maintained, what happens instead is that your right shoulder is in place and continues to move forward with your non-kicking foot,

allowing you to stay in line with the ball. Think of hitting up to the top of the target and your follow through should take you directly in line, through the tee, to the posts finishing with your chest pointing directly at the target. Another way of thinking about the strong body position on impact with the ball is having your chest towards the tee. So keep the chest to the tee coming up to the kick, chest to the tee as the kicking occurs, chest to the tee after the kick and as you lift your head to see where the ball is travelling your chest will naturally turn to face the target.

So I'll take you through one of my kicks. I take 4 steps back from the ball in line with the centre of the posts then 5 steps across and 1 in; that gives me roughly 45 degrees. I like to be a little bit further round than 45 degrees, a bit more narrow. Now I can imagine that strong position and already feel it: chest to the

tee, toe pointed, hard foot, quad doing all the work. I relax my breathing, focusing on the exact point I'm going to strike (just the near panel's side of the stitching, one third of the way up the ball) and then tracing it back up the imaginary wire to the black dot I am aiming at, then from the black dot back down. Now I've got my line. I tend to clasp my hands

Remember to land on your kicking foot to maximise power through the ball

HOW TO PLAY RUGBY MY WAY

in front of me as I'm creating this mental picture. I can't really explain why but it seems to help me. Then I come in towards the ball, concentrating on achieving the strong position, chest to the tee, right side forward, hard foot coming in on that inside panel, the exact point. The strike is hit up through the line of the ball, and I try to force my body towards the target, adding weight to the kick, and hopefully with a balanced finish sending it along the imaginary wire from my tee to the black dot.

## Practice drill

You are on your own with this skill I'm afraid. Practising kicking over a goal post is obviously essential – you need to feel comfortable with the height as well as the direction. But you don't always need posts. Dead aim is a very important concept, which is being very very specific in what you aim for when you're kicking. See the exact point of the ball you're going to hit and from that point trace the line to the top of the target and back down. That's dead aim. Seeing the exact black dot I want to hit on the target back down to the ball. That black dot can be anywhere – that's why you

## Best in the Business

don't always need access to posts to practise. I sometimes use a black dot on a metal bar dead in front of me and I try to get as close to it as I can. At other times I aim for just one post, it could be a telegraph pole or a tree. Then, when it comes to kicking though posts, all you have to do is put your black dot right in the middle of the posts and aim for that.

Dave Alred is the best kicking coach in the world. It looks and sounds as though he is using a different ball. Sometimes it is just great to sit back and watch him perform.

## Top tip

Goal kicking is great because it is the same in practice as in a game situation, so practise well and give yourself the best chance of putting it over.

# Drop kicking

# Drop kicking

The drop kick is very similar to a place kick except the drop kick is not a dead-ball situation and is therefore much harder. It can be a very powerful attacking option that puts points on the board, especially if you are facing a well-organised defence that you are having trouble breaking through and they are not allowing you to get quick ball with which to put together decent attacks.

Communication is a key element of drop kicks – you need to position yourself correctly with sufficient depth to give yourself time 'in the pocket' as it is known – and your team mates need to know that you are ready to receive the ball in order to make the kick. Obviously you need to be within range of the posts!

## How to do it

There are several variables that can affect the kick, such as the way the ball is dropped, who's charging at you, the turf underneath, how it bounces etc. With the drop kick, however, every principle is exactly the same as a goal kick, body at 45 degrees to the target, chest to the ball, hard foot, hit up, power through the ball in the line you want it to travel.

## Alred's expertise

Drop kicks need to be done in a very sharp but controlled motion. There is not much time with defenders charging towards you. By spreading your fingers on the ball and lowering your hands towards the ground before the drop you can achieve more control and more chance of a good nose-to-nose execution, which means the ball comes off the ground straight back towards your hands, therefore improving the likelihood of a good contact. The contact should be immediately after the ball has bounced. It is a half volley and the sound rhythm is a 'Ka-boom'.

If you are receiving a pass and are planning to kick there's no point in standing with your feet facing the passer in order to catch the ball because when it arrives you still need to turn 45 degrees in order to get into position to execute the kick. Too slow, too much movement, too much room for error. For a drop goal attempt, you need to be standing at the correct 45-degree angle ready to kick before the ball gets to you.

Imagine the clock face again. The target is at 12 o'clock and therefore, for a right-footed drop kick, the correct angle is for you to be facing between the 1 and the 2 (at half past 1 if you like). Slightly further round than you would be for a spiral kick. For a left-footed kick, you should be facing towards half past 10 (between 10 and 11). On receiving the pass while facing in the correct direction, you must

drop the ball vertically directly between your legs. This is slightly different from the technique of punting because with a drop kick, your body has to move further round the clock face in order for the leg to be able to swing through the correct path, helping the ball to connect with the right part of the foot. Dropping the ball directly between your legs will automatically put you in a strong and effective position for kicking, as I discussed in the place kicking chapter (i.e. hard foot, chest facing the ball, opposite shoulder forward, focused on where you are going to make contact with the ball).

However, if you drop the ball further forward alongside your front (non-kicking) foot instead of between your legs, what will happen is that you will automatically bring your foot round to meet the ball. It will also

HOW TO PLAY RUGBY MY WAY

mean that you are forced to rotate your chest and shoulder round to bring about this change in position. Your chest will no longer be on the ball and your posture here is weak, because the opposite shoulder is pulling away from the kick and dragging the leg into a C-shape©. You are liable to either come away from the ball, (a slice), or if you are able to get round the back of the ball, you're going to hook it in the direction the leg is swinging. Both options are bad. And there will be far less power transferred through the ball in the desired direction because you will be attempting to kick with a C-shape© swing, not using your strong quad muscle.

If you drop the ball on your kicking foot, slightly behind yourself, your chest needs to come right round, this time in the opposite direction causing a folding at the hips and waist – not a big, tall, strong position. You

are having to collect the ball, and you're going to lose all your power and comfort.

So the ball drop is right in the middle of your legs, hands either side of the ball with spread fingers so you're in total control. Think about the drop by the expression 'nose-to-nose' – the nose of the ball bounces back up directly towards your nose. That's a good execution. Keep your head down and focus intently on exactly where your foot is going to connect, and strike the ball exactly at the moment it touches the ground. Keeping your head down also helps you be deliberate and precise therefore cutting out the distraction of the defence charging at you.

The rest is simple as with goal kicking; opposite shoulder forward, hit up to the top of the target with a hard foot. Shift your weight forward towards the posts and be balanced in your finished follow through.

## Alred's expertise

When kicking restarts, when of course you have much more time because it's a dead ball situation. Try and drop the ball as you would when kicking for goal, i.e. positioned between the legs and nose-to-nose. Allow more time for the ball to bounce back up from the ground. This allows the foot to get underneath the ball and connect with the underside of the point. Rather than a half volley it is a bounce hit. This kick is a cross between a drop kick and a small drop punt, which pings off the top of the foot. Hit up with your leg through to the top of the target with your opposite shoulder forward to complete the kick and keep your balance. Practice by giving the ball as much time to bounce as possible – test yourself. The nose-to-nose drop is very important here. This kick is used to restart the game so the more height on the kick, the more time the chasers have to cover the minimum 10 yards to recover the ball.

HOW TO PLAY RUGBY MY WAY

## Practice drill

It is the fact the ball is kicked just as it connects with the ground that makes these kicks unique and difficult, so it is important to get used to that timing. Stand front on similar to how you would for a drop punt, drop the ball dead straight. Repeating this a number of times will help you get accustomed to how the ball will look as it hits the ground. Once you can do that, remain front on and practise kicking the ball, just on the point of impact with the ground using the top of your foot. Be sure to kick right through the ball, just to get used to how it feels to kick a ball as it hits the floor. Once you are comfortable with that, you can turn your body to the correct position (between 1 and 2 on the clock, or between 10 and 11) and follow the place kicking fundamentals – strong position, hard foot, now using the knuckle just above your instep, shoulder

## Alred's expertise

When drop kicking for goal, do not try to hit the ball too hard. Use your body weight and the power of your J-shape© leg swing. Make sure you connect with the ball as soon as it hits the ground. It is vital that you shunt your bodyweight towards the posts whilst hitting up. Keep that in mind and you will be able to get enough power without having to swing your leg too quickly, which introduces room for error through lack of balance and control.

forward, chest to the ball, focus on where you're going to hit the ball, hit up to the target, continue the follow through and send the ball along the wire finishing with your chest to the target. Have one of your team mates pass the ball to you as if he were a scrum half. This will give you excellent practice in perfoming in realistic game conditions – because the pass won't always be perfect! And to add to the realism, have other team mates try to charge your kick down, using a tackle shield.

## Best in the Business

Rob Andrew – under pressure he always knew how to keep his head and his shape to make the big kicks.

# Looking after your body

# Looking after your body

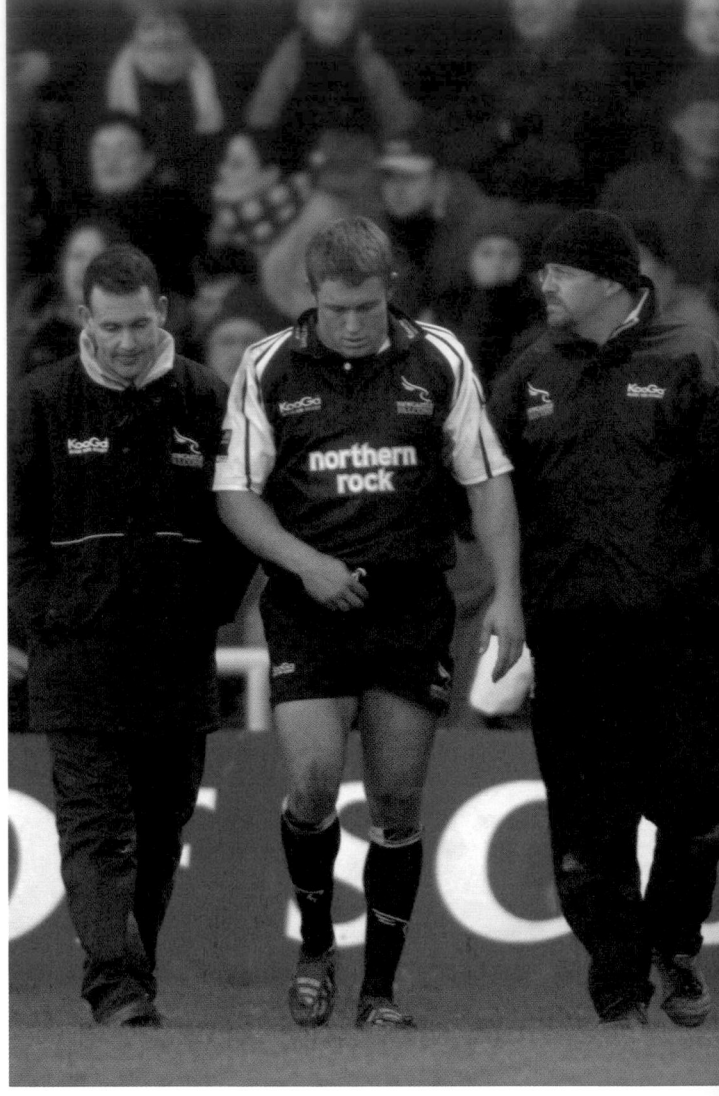

In rugby, injuries are a fact of life, I'm afraid. It is a precarious sport. Blackie calls them 'Industrial Hazards' and he is right. There are many things you can do to mitigate the likelihood of an injury occurring – proper training, building up your strength through exercise, ensuring you are performing the skills such as kicking and tackling correctly with a good technique – but ultimately, rugby is a contact sport and injuries will happen.

All of the injuries I have had are as a result of being hit in a tackle or tackling someone. I am always trying to get my techniques spot on during game play – for instance tackling in the way I described earlier in that skills chapter – but people move off line and change direction suddenly or people move at different speeds, so it is not always going to be text-book style out

there. It is because some of the players are so powerful, and that it is impossible to adjust how you fall in a tackle sometimes, that trauma injuries occur to the structure of the body. You can break bones, dislocate things, or you can damage ligaments and muscles. That's what happened to me. My training and preparation have always been properly planned and thought out – it is just that sometimes you can be in the wrong place at the wrong time.

So don't despair if you do pick up the odd contact-related injury. Everyone does. It doesn't mean you are doing something wrong. What is important is that you get the proper medical attention that the injury requires, you work hard to get yourself back to peak fitness again, and you approach the injury with the correct mental outlook. That's what this section is all about – how you deal with injuries.

The one thing I will say, however, is that regardless of what injuries I have had, and may have again, I wouldn't change my style of play. Your style is what makes you you. The way you play is an expression of your own individuality, and I'd hate to have to tamper with that. I think I'd be tampering with myself as a person. Being injured has also made me even more aware of how much I love my rugby and now that I know what it is like to be side-lined I am determined that I will make the best use of my time that I possibly can when I am playing. That gives me a very positive attitude which helps me in my game. So a lot of good can come out of injuries!

HOW TO PLAY RUGBY MY WAY

There are times when you have to knuckle down, put your head down and just say 'this needs to be done'. But never have I had to question the sacrifices in terms of their worth. I've just got to make sure I look back on this period as the most fruitful part of my life.

## My history of injuries

I've always had neck problems. Playing cricket, every now and again, my neck would just go. I have dealt with painful episodes from playing rugby since I was about 14 years old. But I didn't suffer any major injuries until a good few years into my professional career. The first major game-affecting injury was in the autumn of 2002 when I damaged the AC joint in my shoulder (a fairly common injury for athletes involved in collision sports) keeping me out for nine weeks. Then I was fine again all the way through 2003 and into the World Cup in Australia where I did hurt my neck a couple of times, but that was par for the course, and something I had already taken for granted.

When I came back from Australia I played against Northampton and after about 55 minutes, I injured my neck badly, losing the ability to work any of the muscles in my upper right arm. I don't think it was a case of the way I was playing. It was a combination of factors:

a bit of bad luck in a couple of collisions, maybe the fact that I had neck problems at a younger age, maybe even the number of times I'd hurt my neck and then got up and played on.

That injury took me one operation and nine or ten months to get over. Then, coming back from that, I injured my right arm because of the subsequent muscle loss from being out for all those weeks, forcing me to take another break; about eight weeks this time, because the pain was just too much to deal with. It was affecting the way I was approaching playing rugby. I was back for a few games until I turned out of a tackle during a match against Perpignan in the European Cup, my studs got caught, and everyone piled into the side of my knee. I didn't want to come off the field and so I thought 'Okay, I'll have a little walk and a jog to shake it off,' at which point my knee just completely collapsed.

I went for a scan that night and had a massive panic attack. I was really worried that something very serious had gone wrong. Fortunately it was only a tear of the medial ligament in my left knee – bad enough but not career-threatening. I recovered once again and came back to play against Harlequins. I was really enjoying myself when all of a sudden, while challenging for the ball on the floor after making a tackle I was hit from the side and I heard my knee pop – properly this time. My knee was moving around way too much and I was pretty sure I must have done real damage and ruptured the whole thing.

But I was lucky, I hadn't. But I'd torn it again and it proved to be about another six to eight weeks off. I came back from that and played two Tests on the Lions tour and hurt my neck in the second one, but it wasn't too serious. It just took a good bang which meant that the nerve was swollen for about two weeks; but it certainly didn't stop me meeting up and training with the Hotshots.

## Dealing with injuries

I hate being injured. Of course I do. Everyone does. I find it so frustrating to watch the game

I love being played by others and not being in a position to join in, not being able to fight for my team, my goals and my ambitions, not being able to express myself or show my team mates how hard I've been working or how much I care that we are able to win. But any sportsperson has to accept that there is a fair chance that they will have to go through that experience at some stage.

The key is how you deal with it, and to me, the only way you can is to think, 'All I can do is go away and work and try and come back stronger, so that when I am back doing what

I love, I'll be even better than I was previously.' Adopting that attitude gives you the motivation to get yourself fit again – and when you make it back, it can be a huge point of satisfaction. You set yourself a target and you achieved it. The mental strength you gain from going through that experience, being forced to take it on the chin but coming through in the end, can be fantastic. I'd like to think that I've been made a stronger person because of this, and a more motivated person because I have set my new goals and am desperate to achieve them.

Adopting the right mental attitude is critical and I also think that it is important to get away from rugby for a bit. In hindsight, I wish I'd taken a few weeks off after some of my injuries, but at least I did manage to escape from games to an extent. I didn't go and watch all the Newcastle matches because I couldn't handle that. I couldn't cope being reminded of the fact I wasn't out there playing all the time. So I decided not to go, and that was the right decision.

Not dwelling on what you are missing out on is the key. It wasn't that I was not supporting the team – I did that all week at training and with good luck messages. There is no doubt that injury tests you mentally as well as physically. If, when you come back, you're mentally exhausted and haven't got the energy or enthusiasm to focus on your game, you can quickly become depressed or burnt out.

Physically recovering from the injury is one thing – actually getting back into the swing of playing again is another thing altogether. If you are out of the game for a while, when you do make it back the whole thing can seem very unfamiliar and you lose your innate ability to deal with pressure. I remember during one of my periods out, watching Newcastle play in the Powergen Cup in front of 50,000 people and thinking, 'How can they possibly cope with all those nerves'. I had to remind myself that I'd played through a World Cup final. But I was finding it hard to imagine myself out there on the pitch.

What you have got to realise is that it takes a lot out of you to deal with different injuries and preparing yourself mentally – from the time of the injury itself, through the recuperation, right up to the moment you set foot again on a rugby pitch – is just as important at the physical rehabilitation. You have got

## Blackie's secrets

Initially Jonny will feel very down about an injury. Then he gathers his strength, appraises the situation very objectively and tries to get the right people to tell him how things stand in terms of the severity of the injury and how quickly he can begin the rehabilitation process. By the time that process starts Jonny will be back on top form from a mental standpoint. That is very important. Being positive and optimistic helps the healing process.

Working with Jonny, we set a goal in mind and push on towards it. And it won't be just getting back to where he was before the injury – he aims to be better than that. That's what stimulates him enormously, finding that his levels have gone up.

to set yourself ambitious but achievable targets, you have got to visualise yourself playing again and keep positively reinforcing the message to yourself that when you do get back you will know how to handle it and you will in fact be better than you were before the injury occurred.

Retain your self-belief and faith in the part of your natural rugby-playing ability. Once that whistle goes, you know you will be fine because you badly want to win – you don't want to let anyone down – you have done your practice and preparation and you have done it so many times before.

## Food and diet

When I was younger I never really thought about what I ate. To be honest, I was so active that I never seemed to stop. I was doing one sport, then off to another one, and then straight on to another one after that. I ate fairly healthily, because my parents were pretty good about making sure we had a decent diet – lots of chicken, potatoes and vegetables, lots of vegetables.

As I've grown older I've become even more healthy and it's actually helped me be more adventurous. Before, I was a very fussy eater, but now I've realised how much good food there is out there that I could be eating so I've branched out into fish, for instance, and other vegetables that I wouldn't necessarily have liked before. Now I go out of my way to find shops that sell different foods, and I find that really helps me to enjoy my eating, because I'm trying new things and seeking out alternatives.

Diets are very personal as every body is so different in what it needs and how much energy it uses daily. With a lot of these things, if you can just understand what your body needs and how much energy comes from which foods, you can make your own meal plans to suit your own lifestyle.

## The basics

Diet is about having enough energy to do the things you want to do and eating the right balance of foods and liquids to keep your body working and renewing itself. Your principal source of energy will come from carbohydrates, foods like cereals, bread, pasta, potatoes and rice as these all release

# I eat loads of meat because it's got lots of protein in it and it helps you rebuild your muscles. After training, your muscles take a bit of a hammering, so you need that.

energy. Wholemeal bread, wholemeal pasta and wholemeal rice release energy more gradually than white versions of the same food because they are complex carbohydrates, not simple, and therefore take longer to break down, releasing energy bit by bit. This is good for you because it can keep you going for a long time. I tend to start my day with bowls of cereal and brown toast to kickstart my body so it gets enough energy for my morning training.

You also need to make sure you are getting enough protein as this is part of building muscles and helps all your cells function and your body work the way it should. You can find protein in a huge variety of foods like eggs, meat, nuts, beans, lentils and so on. The key is getting good amounts of protein into every meal if you can, to keep up with the constant regeneration your body needs. For example, for breakfast I often eat an eggwhite omelette, which is low in fat but high in protein because the yolks are taken out.

# The harder I practise, the luckier I get. I believe that totally.

Fruit and vegetables are essential as they give you the vital vitamins and minerals you need, sometimes as well as the right kinds of carbohydrates. I tend to eat a lot of vegetables at night rather than huge amounts of potatoes and bread.

This might sound strange but lastly, you must balance your diet out with the right type of fat which you get from foods like nuts and certain fish. You must be careful not to eat too much fat in general, including red meat and fried food, as this will only serve to put excess weight on you, making you feel unhealthy and slowing you down on the pitch.

If you can tailor your diet to include a bit of all of the above every day, you should have a balanced diet, with enough energy and fuel for rebuilding muscles; vital for a growing rugby player. When training, however, you must realise how much this impacts on your body. It is vital to have enough energy to train but also to put it straight back afterwards by using sports drinks like Lucozade or carbohydrate snacks. When you train, especially weight training, your muscles are actually broken down by the strenuous activity. If supplied with the right amounts of protein and energy from carbohydrates very soon after training is finished, the muscles rebuild bigger and stronger. If not fed with sufficient protein you will not add bulk or become stronger. Make sure you eat a lot of protein and refuel your energy levels after your heavy training sessions or your hard work will be wasted.

It is also important that you remember to do two more things. One is to always drink enough. So loads of water, fluids, and around training, isotonic sports drinks. It's really good to drink before, during and after your training, as well as throughout the day. The second point is to make sure you don't deprive yourself of too much. If you have a healthy lifestyle and exercise regularly, get out and about and you're always active and burning energy, and you make sure your calories in are matching your calories burned, then you don't need to worry. Never be afraid to eat the things you like eating

every now and then. You know, if you want to eat puddings or chocolates occasionally, then as long as they're in moderation, that's absolutely fine. I think things like that make sense and it's really just a question of being level-headed. We say that eating well makes you feel good and it improves the quality of life. Looking good helps you to feel good.

## New foods

I think it's important not to get stuck in a food 'rut'. You will get to know what you like as you get older but I really advise you to keep trying new foods and recipes. I like talking to other people about their diets as I believe taking advice from them helps me a lot, because sometimes you can get a bit daunted or bored by the requirements of eating healthily. At the start you might think, 'Oh well, you know, foods that are healthy taste very plain, or aren't very nice'; or that tasty, rich, exciting foods are bad for you. But that's not necessarily true. I think you need to understand that some of the best things to eat are actually healthy anyway.

Learning to cook and testing out great new recipes from friends and books has been a massive learning curve for me, which I've really enjoyed. I recently went and made some turkey burgers for the barbecue we were having at home. I just took some lean turkey mince with onions and a couple of egg whites cracked in to hold it all together (all good protein), and just stuck it on the barbecue. You couldn't ask for anything better and it was delicious, especially if you want to add in some herbs too. There's no real fat in it, there's loads of protein, and I always think that anything

made on the barbecue tastes great and seems more fun to cook. I've also realised that the way you combine ingredients can make a difference to what you eat as certain mixtures of foods make a meal even more healthy. For example, I learned recently that if you're going to have wholegrain rice for a meal, you can mix some peas in with it – these can be chick peas or any small peas – and the rice and those peas together combine to form really good protein. This also works with soya beans or lentils. You might be surprised at what food actually has the elements that your body needs.

I've got to make sure that when I go out there and play, I've got a smile on my face. Or if it's not on my face, it's just below the surface waiting to come out because that's when I play at my best.

For me, the key is understanding – understanding which types of foods are good for your body, and which types aren't so good – rather than saying 'you must never eat that'. If you're going out for dinner, it's not a case of saying, as some do, 'Oh, you should never eat this or you should never eat an Indian take away as it's all bad for you.' You can work out what you can have. Decide what is going to be a good dish for you – maybe something which has lots of vegetables or something which doesn't come in a creamy sauce and which hasn't been fried. The Indian-style oven-cooked or grilled meats are fantastic and should not be missed.

Therefore, when you do go to restaurants or even abroad on holiday and you want to order local food, then great. Go ahead. You know what sort of things to look out for, and that allows you to make the most of foreign cuisine and try new foods. And at the same time, you're not going to feel too guilty after you finish eating.

Team
Wilkinson

# Team Wilkinson

## The Importance of Family to Success

**W**ithout doubt my family has been the centrepiece of everything I've been able to achieve. It's amazing what a selfish life I've lived and I've realised that I spend a lot of my time on myself: I spend my time kicking and practising, and yet I never look at that as selfish when I'm actually doing it. It's only when I sit back and think about it that I realise I've been able to go through my life and not see it as self-centred because I've had a group of people around me who have never questioned it – never questioned whether they should be giving me the support, never questioned whether they should be driving me 40 miles across the country, even just to take me to practice because I'm not happy with the way things are going. Or they'll spend time with me sorting out my schedule, like my dad does, making sure that I've got time to do all my practice. And if I need to be somewhere, he'll be right there to take me, or he'll make sure that I can get to where I need to be. My brother is the same, always there for me. When I need him to do some defensive work after we've had an exhausting training session, he's hurting, and yet he'll just run for me while I practise my tackling – and I'll do the same for him.

I try as hard as I can to pay them back, but sometimes I'm not in a position where I can do that in a similar vein. I really don't have the time where I can be there every time for Mum and Dad yet. I can't really give them as much as I'd love to, as much as they've given me, because of the situation I'm in. My time seems to be all taken up and I have a busy life, but I try and pay that back with a certain amount of respect to my parents and brother with the way I lead my life: my values, my ethics and my morals and the image I portray to the younger generation.

## Best buddies – Jonny and Sparks

My brother and I are very close in our relationship. We're at ease with each other and always have been. We've always played, more or less, on the same team, despite the fact that he's a year and a bit older than me. This was up until we went to different schools, when I was about 14 and my brother was about 16. He had finished his exams and the school we were at closed down. I went to one school and he went to a different one, which was more or less when we first split. Then Sparks went to university, and I finished my schooling and came up to Newcastle to play rugby. As soon as he finished university, he

came up and joined me which was around one year after I'd got there. We started sharing a house then and we've lived together for the past seven or eight years, and now he plays for the Falcons too, it couldn't have worked out better.

We spend so much time together that you'd think it would be a recipe for disaster, when actually it just continues to make things better. It's his unselfishness which really makes it work. But we both have an ability to feed off each other, to understand when one needs a bit of time, or needs cheering up, or needs to be kept busy, or needs a bit of a rest; it's a key part of our relationship. So if he's not feeling his best or he's feeling a bit down, I'll go out and make sure that I get the food and sort the evening out, and he'll repay the favour when I'm not feeling 100 per cent.

We seem to know each other so well, that it's been a massive influence on the way that I've been able to attack my rugby. And the good thing is now, when I attack it, I'm doing it with him as well, so it's a nice balance. But it's good to know that you have someone like that who's got your best interest at heart, and our feelings for each other are totally unconditional. Regardless of whatever happened in life, I know he'd be right there for me and I'd do the same for him.

He's also a great support in just helping me deal with things. I'm quite an intense individual. Intense in that when I'm focused on something, I'm fairly obsessive, and my problem is that sometimes I can't shift that. I do think that if Sparks hadn't been around, I don't know quite where I'd be now. It's so difficult to switch off sometimes, for example if I've played a game in the evening, I often won't go to bed until 4 o'clock in the morning. It's not from going out or anything, it's just that I can't switch off: I'm constantly thinking about all the things I'd wish I'd done differently, all the things I can't believe I did, or things I know I can do so much better, and yet, in the game I didn't get right. Those things, they're like little demons that sit on my shoulder and just natter at me the whole time. I sometimes find it very difficult to get away from those feelings, because, as I'm a bit of a perfectionist, everything that's not perfectly right is very wrong to me.

Sparks has this ability to just crack a joke at the right moment. When I'm going over something in my head and trying to work out what I did wrong, he'll make me laugh which will then make me completely forget whatever it was I was thinking about and why it was wrong. It also makes me realise quite quickly how much more there is to life than just going over your past mistakes. He gives me that balance. He is my release from the fact that when I am not totally happy with the way I feel I have played I can go a long time without seeing anyone. I can get quite isolated and spend a lot of time on my own and go into hiding a bit, and no one knows me better than my brother and how to get me out of that.

## The ultimate support network – Mum and Dad

Having Mum and Dad up in Newcastle is great. They live pretty close by and we spend a lot of time together: having barbecues in the summer, or just catching up during the week. To be in a situation where sometimes my dad will phone me and say, 'What are you up to? We're having a bit of a barbecue, do you want to come round?', is a great position to be in, to be able to take that break. If you've been on the field all day and really getting stuck into your training and things

That's me at the front with a bunch of mates. Sparks is at the back – perhaps showing how many tries he's expecting to score in his career

HOW TO PLAY RUGBY MY WAY

are going well or things aren't going so well, to just have that barbecue and switch off is a huge relief.

I also have a working relationship with my dad and my mum. Mum looks after the charity side of things and any mail I get. Dad is more on the business side, managing my time and where I need to be and taking care of organisation. So I meet up with them on a regular basis. Again, if you were in a situation where you realised how much time you spent with certain people, that you spent basically all your life with them, you think that you must come to blows, but again very, very rarely does anything cause an argument. I think it's the support side again. I think the strength of our relationships almost gives us the knowledge that everything is going to be alright, be it on the rugby field in front of 80,000, be it training in front of no one, or be it on my way to a sponsorship appearance.

There are of course times when you're not quite sure how you feel about everything when you're nervous or insecure, but you know that it's going to be alright because you've got these special people round you and if it all went to pot that they'd step up and help you through anything

## What Sparks thinks

I think you either get brothers who don't get on with each other or brothers who are really tight friends. I've been very lucky as I've just always been close to Jonny. We very rarely argue and never really fought. A 19-month age difference is a good one. If you're into the same things, you can do them together, because it's not too big an age gap to be a drag, where one is able to do something and the other can't. We've always knocked around together both at home and on the pitch.

One of Mum and Dad's rules was 'no ball in the house', so to get away from that, we made our own rugby balls out of toilet rolls filled with tissue, posts out of paper and then had kicking competitions in the house. So, we weren't breaking the rules because there was no ball. If they had said 'no tissue rolls in the house'... But we've always been close with Mum and Dad. We've always been more of a four than a two with Mum and Dad joining in whatever we've been doing, and that's still the case. There's nothing that the family, as a whole, do for Jonny that he couldn't do on his own. It's just that we tend to do it a bit better than he does, and he's more than happy now to let us get on with it.

Rugby has cemented our relationship even further because now, playing on the same team, we can share in the same experiences. I think that it's the same for everyone. If you go through things together, they tend to bring you tighter. It's a massive boost for me to know that I'm going out onto the pitch and that I can look to my side, and my brother's standing there and it's going to work. He's at my back and he's looking out for me and vice versa. In the last couple of years I've played when he's been smashed up, so I'm looking forward to the opportunity to actually get back on the pitch with him and to enjoy that side of things.

I think living and working together also lets Jonny chill out a bit. A lot of the guys on the team actually live very nearby to the club. For them, it's just a case of getting to training, then when they finish, they can pop home for a bit, chill out and come back if we've got training in the afternoon. Jonny and I have ended up in a situation where we're living a bit further away, so we'll be out from the house for the whole day and when you do get home it's a massive relief and you think, 'Right,

That's me in the middle - about to get stuck in for Farnham

# Fame was the last thing on my mind when I started playing the game.

let's do something a bit different.' This is where the table tennis, the music and watching loads of movies and the various other fads and things we've been through, come into play. I think now he's trying to create the world's most incredible basketball net out of something or other. To be honest, I've no idea what he's trying to build it out of. But he has these little schemes and he's always got something he wants to recreate like he did when we were about 10. He's just going through his memories and trying to bring them back now that he's 26.

## What Dad thinks

As a family we are close. We've always enjoyed the boys' company; we've always liked being with them, working with them, and vice versa. They used to come to my cricket and rugby games and there was never any pushing them into it or anything like that, it was just something they picked up and enjoyed from watching.

We try to support Jonny and Sparks as much as we can. I'm a great believer that if somebody wants to concentrate on something and be good at it, if you can relieve them of all the other pressures, then that's going to help. Just let them concentrate on whatever they want to do. So we've always tried to assist both of them. This process sort of finished up by moving to the northeast three years ago to be near them, and really just alleviating all the outside pressures, allowing them to concentrate on what they do best. It's a short career.

Jonny and Sparks have a great relationship. They've always been very close, which has been ideal, because they've always had somebody to play with. They're 19 months apart, so when they were younger, and it was raining, you didn't have to worry about getting other kids round to the house. They're very supportive of one another. They always have been. There's never any competitive spirit between them. If they play table tennis, or tennis, then it's just a warm-up for three hours. They don't want to or need to demonstrate who might be better than the other. It's very much a practice. We're very proud of both of them.

# I'm just trying to do my bit for rugby, to make it a better sport.

## What Mum thinks

If you've got children you love them to death and you're proud of them. We've got two children, we love them to death, we're proud of them. And if you can have a relationship with your children like we do, and the fun we have, then that's the best. You can't ask for anything else. And that's the reward as well, for what you put into your children. That's magic for me.

Sparks and Jonny work for each other. Jonny can be very focused and at times under quite a lot of pressure which he puts on himself. I think one of our main jobs is that if things don't go right, or Jonny feels that things haven't gone right, we're here to take all the stick really. I just try and tell a joke or Sparks can come in with his little one-liners or just do something stupid, and the whole situation just relaxes. But it works the other way too. Sparks has worries as well – for example he has been taking the number 10 position for Newcastle when Jonny's been injured and that's been a huge pressure for Sparks. Jonny's been there the whole time talking him through and preparing him, and they bounce off each other. But together, they are terrific fun. We all enjoy each other's company.

As a baby, Jonny was an absolute nightmare. Even when he was just crawling he would constantly chase us round and round the house. It was very tiring. He only slept through the night for the first time at the age of 8. Obviously in the latter years it was easier because he could read or have a TV in his room, but it was certainly a case of never a dull moment.

It was quite a learning curve for Jonny when he moved up to Newcastle at 18. It was also, from the domestic side, quite a jump for him, because, bearing in mind the hours he spent

The classic team photo of the Farnham under 8s, Sparks taking care of his team mate with a hug

at school, and the weekends with sport and everything, he didn't actually get involved in day-to day things like shopping or looking after himself. He even once asked me if he had to take his passport with him as ID for when he bought something at the shop with a cheque!

You must be able to stop what you're doing, look at everything and think – 'am I having fun?'

# The Hotshots

## Selection

To be chosen for the Hotshots programme, each entrant had to send in a video of themselves playing rugby and explain why they wanted to be picked for the show. When the BBC told me there were over 1,000 videos of 10–14 year olds kicking, passing, tackling and running with the ball, I was amazed and completely unprepared for the quality of the players. It was outstanding. After the longlist of 20 had been compiled, fellow internationals Jeremy Guscott and Jonathan Davies had the unenviable job of trying to get that figure down. At the try-out day they fairly put them through their paces at Bath and unbelievably got the list down to 10 future stars: eight boys and two girls.

## The Hotshots

Meeting the Hotshots was a joy. When they came up to Newcastle for the filming there was a great cross-section. Lots of different personalities, but they were all hugely friendly and seemed to get on very well. And they turned up each day exploding with energy; the enthusiasm was incredible. The way in which they attacked every single situation, the way that they sat and stared and watched when I was training with Blackie, the way that they really fired into my brother and I when we were answering some non-rugby ques-tions. They were also able to understand the values that we were talking about like focus, stamina and motivation which are necessary to be a good player. A bunch of young guys and girls who were just awesome – one of the reasons why this project has made it so easy for me to put something back into the game. You know you are being listened to and you know you will be able to see the results and improvements. I have huge respect for them all and for the way they've been brought up, for the way they are as individuals, the way they care for other people, look out for each other. That's what makes people who play winners anyway.

We had a great time together and it was nice to have such an attentive audience. Despite the tiring nature of the filming, some of them just wanted to get back on the field as soon as they finished the session, to practise some more. I loved it – just the good-naturedness and the way I was given satisfaction because of their willingness and cheery smiles. The thing is you don't get something out of it unless you listen and learn, unless you practise and that's exactly what they all did.

Skill wise, I think every single one of them could be a star. It depends, because a lot of it will be determined by the maturing process over the next few years and also how they find communication and how they build up confidence, self belief and mental and physical strength. There's a couple of leaders in there, people who you'd expect to be captain, but there's also a couple who are honest, and who would give anything: told to go and do this, they go and give 100 per cent. I think that as much as you need leaders, you need enough people at the next level. These are the team mates that will get the job done for you, and no one appreciates that more than myself.

I'm definitely going to keep an eye on them.

Matt Baker and myself with the Hotshots in Newcastle

HOW TO PLAY RUGBY MY WAY

**NAME:** Shannon Davidson
**AGE:** 11
**POSITION:** Prop
**FROM:** Moira, Northern Ireland
**FAVOURITE SPORTSMAN/WOMAN:** Bryn Cunningham and Kelly Holmes
**I HATE...** not playing rugby
**IF I WON THE LOTTERY,**
**I WOULD...** buy a rugby pitch, a horse, and a private jet and I would give some money to Cancer Research

**NAME:** Adam Dearden
**AGE:** 12
**POSITION:** Fly half
**FROM:** Dunblane, Scotland
**FAVOURITE FILM:** Indiana Jones And The Temple of Doom
**IF I WON THE LOTTERY, I WOULD...** make a rugby stadium in my back garden
**FAVOURITE MUSIC:** Peter Kay's '(Is This The Way To) Amarillo'

**NAME:** William Hooley
**AGE:** 11
**POSITION:** Fly half
**FROM:** Cambridge
**FAVOURITE SPORTSMAN/WOMAN:** Jonny Wilkinson and Kelly Holmes
**FAVOURITE BOOK:** a history of rugby
**WHAT I WOULD TAKE ON A DESERT ISLAND...** PlayStation 2

**NAME:** Matthew Mellish
**AGE:** 13
**POSITION:** Scrum half/Fly half
**FROM:** South Shields, Tyne and Wear
**FAVOURITE SPORTSMAN/WOMAN:** Martin Johnson and Marion Jones
**FAVOURITE BOOK:** My World by Jonny Wilkinson
**IF I WON THE LOTTERY, I WOULD...** buy a huge house and put a rugby pitch and posts in my back garden

**NAME:** Jamie Morrish
**AGE:** 13
**POSITION:** Outside centre
**FROM:** Crathes Banchory, Scotland
**FAVOURITE SPORTSMAN/WOMAN:** Tana Umaga and Chris Paterson
**I LOVE ...** eating steak and onion baguettes
**TAKE ON A DESERT ISLAND...** a really big supply of steak and onion sandwiches

**NAME:** Ceri Roberts
**AGE:** 12
**POSITION:** Fly half
**FROM:** Llanelli, Wales
**FAVOURITE SPORTSMAN/WOMAN:** Brian O'Driscoll, Denise Lewis
**I LOVE...** going to sport shops and buying rugby jerseys
**IF I WON THE LOTTERY, I WOULD...** buy a rugby stadium

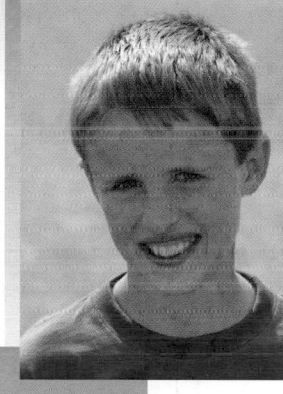

**NAME:** Timothy Small
**AGE:** 12
**POSITION:** Scrum half
**FROM:** Randalstown, Northern Ireland
**FAVOURITE SPORTSMAN:** Brian O'Driscoll
**I LOVE...** my family! And polo-mints
**MY AMBITION IS TO...** be a professional rugby player and play for Ireland

**NAME:** Tilly Vaughan-Fowler
**AGE:** 10
**POSITION:** Fly half
**FROM:** Merton, Oxfordshire
**FAVOURITE BOOK:** the Ikea catalogue
**I HATE...** the Australian team
**FAVOURITE FOOD:** Mum's chocolate brownies

**NAME:** Ben Winstanly
**AGE:** 11
**POSITION:** Fly half
**FROM:** Wigan
**FAVOURITE BOOK:** this one!
**IF I WON THE LOTTERY, I WOULD...** go out all night
**TAKE ON A DESERT ISLAND...** a rugby ball

**NAME:** Sam Womersley
**AGE:** 11
**POSITION:** Scrum half
**FROM:** Mirfield, West Yorkshire
**I HATE...** baked beans
**MY AMBITION IS TO...** lead England out at Twickenham
**FAVOURITE LESSON:** PE and maths

# Jonny's factfile

## MY...

**First trophy:** Farnham under 8s – Horsham tournament in Sussex

**First hero:** Ellery Hanley (below)

**First match watched on TV:** England v Wales in 1989 when England lost after Mike Hall scored in the last minute. I am not sure it was a try!

**First live match:** John Player Cup final Bath v Wasps

**First memory of a sporting event:** 1988 Olympics and Ben Johnson. My dad playing number 8 for Alton

## MY FAVOURITE...

**Book:** Anything by Michael Connolly or Harlan Coben who write detective-based stories

**Film:** The Matrix or The Predator

**Food:** Chicken

**Car:** Mercedes

**Holiday destination:** Spain

**Music:** Oasis

**Actor:** Keanu Reeves

**Actress:** Sandra Bullock

**Other sporting stars:** The late Walter Payton, the American Football running back for the Chicago Bears Michael Jordan and Dominic Wilkins from the National Basketball Association in America

**Children's book:** The BFG by Roald Dahl

**Subject at school:** Chemistry and French

**Piece of advice:** All you have when you leave the game of rugby or even the game of life is your reputation, so do anything you can while you have the chance to build a good one

**Inspiration:** Steve Black (Blackie). Somebody who has always been there for me, who I admire and respect hugely and who has taught me a great deal about values and ethics

**Moment in rugby:** World Cup final and playing with Mark, my brother, for the Falcons

**Other sport:** Table tennis and basketball

**TV programme:** The Simpsons

## MY...

**Life after rugby:** Coaching children and at an elite level. Trying to help sportsmen to deal with professionalism and maybe some travelling, especially to Africa.

**Biggest disappointment in rugby:** Anytime I feel I have underperformed or not had the chance to show what I can do. The recent Lions tour to New Zealand was a good case of not being able to do myself justice.

# Jonny's career

## FOR THE FALCONS

| SEASON | All games* App | All games* Pts | All games* % | League App | League Pts | League % | Cup App | Cup Pts | Cup % | Europe App | Europe Pts | Europe % | CLUB HONOURS |
|---|---|---|---|---|---|---|---|---|---|---|---|---|---|
| 1997-98 | 10+4 | 9 | – | 8+3 | 0 | – | 1 | – | – | 0+1 | 5 | – | Champions |
| 1998-99 | 30 | 352 | 82.1% | 25 | 306 | 81.3% | 5 | 46 | 89.5% | | | | 8th/Cup finalist |
| 1999-00 | 20 | 253 | 79.7% | 13 | 163 | 76.9% | 2 | 20 | 100.0% | 5 | 70 | 80.6% | 9th |
| 2000-01 | 24 | 350 | 83.1% | 15 | 203 | 78.9% | 4 | 77 | 87.1% | 5 | 70 | 89.3% | 6th/Cup winner |
| 2001-02 | 25 | 324 | 84.5% | 17 | 215 | 83.5% | 3 | 47 | 84.2% | 4 | 62 | 87.5% | 6th |
| 2002-03 | 20 | 249 | 81.3% | 16 | 205 | 80.7% | | | | 4 | 48 | 90.5% | 10th |
| 2003-04 | 1 | 9 | 100% | 1 | 9 | 100% | | | | | | | 9th/Cup winner |
| 2004-05 | 12+4 | 183 | 78.4% | 10+2 | 150 | 75.8% | 0+1 | 5 | 66.7% | 1+1 | 17 | 100.0% | 7th |
| **TOTALS** | **142+8** | **1733** | **82.0%** | **105+5** | **1251** | **80.0%** | **15+1** | **195** | **87.5%** | **19+2** | **272** | **87.3%** | |

* including playoff matches

## FOR ENGLAND AND THE LIONS

| SEASON | England App | W | D | L | Pts | % | British & Irish Lions App | W | D | L | Pts | % | INTERNATIONAL HONOURS |
|---|---|---|---|---|---|---|---|---|---|---|---|---|---|
| 1998 | 2+1 | 1 | 0 | 2 | – | – | | | | | | | Five Nations runner-up |
| 1999 | 10+1 | 7 | 0 | 4 | 171 | 76.7% | | | | | | | Five Nations runner-up/RWC quarter-final |
| 2000 | 9 | 8 | 0 | 1 | 156 | 79.4% | | | | | | | Six Nations winner |
| 2001 | 7 | 6 | 0 | 1 | 131 | 81.4% | 3 | 1 | 0 | 2 | 36 | 57.1% | Six Nations winner |
| 2002 | 8 | 7 | 0 | 1 | 126 | 87.8% | | | | | | | Six Nations runner-up |
| 2003 | 14 | 14 | 0 | 0 | 233 | 83.9% | | | | | | | RWC winner, Grand Slam winner |
| 2004 | | | | | | | | | | | | | |
| 2005 | | | | | | | 2 | 0 | 0 | 2 | 11 | 66.7% | |
| **TOTALS** | **50+2** | **43** | **0** | **9** | **817** | **80.9%** | **5** | **1** | **0** | **4** | **47** | **59.2%** | |

**Key:** App = number of matches started; plus replacement appearances denoted by +
Pts = points scored
% = kicking accuracy: number of successful attempts divided by total kicks at goal

## TOP PREMIERSHIP POINTS SCORERS 1997-2005

| | | |
|---|---|---|
| **1251** | **Jonny Wilkinson** | **Newcastle Falcons** |
| 1243 | Tim Stimpson | Newcastle/Leicester/Leeds |
| 1238 | Paul Grayson | Northampton |
| 1053 | Barry Everitt | London Irish |
| 882 | Alex King | London Wasps |
| 870 | Andy Goode | Leicester/Saracens |
| 862 | Kenny Logan | London Wasps |
| 860 | Paul Burke | Bristol/Harlequins |
| 840 | Charlie Hodgson | Sale Sharks |

## BEST PREMIERSHIP KICKERS 1997-2005

| | | |
|---|---|---|
| 81.08% | John Schuster | Harlequins |
| 80.77% | Henry Honiball | Bristol |
| **80.00%** | **Jonny Wilkinson** | **Newcastle Falcons** |
| 80.00% | Jon Callard | Bath |
| 78.80% | Mark Van Gisbergen | London Wasps |
| 78.26% | Jannie De Beer | London Scottish/Saracens |
| 78.20% | Jarrod Cunningham | London Irish |
| 78.16% | Jon Preston | Bath |

## TOP TEST MATCH POINTS SCORERS OF ALL TIME

| | | |
|---|---|---|
| 1049 | Neil Jenkins | Wales |
| 1010 | Diego Dominguez | Argentina/Italy |
| 967 | Andrew Mehrtens | New Zealand |
| 911 | Michael Lynagh | Australia |
| 878 | Matthew Burke | Australia |
| **817** | **Jonny Wilkinson** | **England** |
| 667 | Gavin Hastings | Scotland |
| 645 | Grant Fox | New Zealand |
| 590 | Hugo Porta | Argentina/South America |
| 587 | Nicky Little | Fiji |
| 542 | David Humphreys | Ireland |
| 539 | Percy Montgomery | South Africa |
| 525 | Ronan O'Gara | Ireland |

# JONNY'S MATCH HIGHS

**Most points in a game:** 35 - ENGLAND v Italy at Twickenham (Six Nations Championship), 17 February 2001

**Most tries in a game:** 2 – NEWCASTLE v Northampton at Kingston Park (Premiership), 15 November 1998 and 2 – NEWCASTLE v Bedford at Kingston Park (Premiership), 27 February 2000

**Most conversions in a game:** 13 – ENGLAND v United States (Twickenham), 21 August 1999

**Most penalty goals in a game:** 8 ENGLAND v South Africa at Bloemfontein, 24 June 2000 (England all time record) and 8 – NEWCASTLE v Wasps at Kingston Park (Premiership), 1 September 2002

**Most drop goals in a game:** 3 – ENGLAND v France at Sydney (World Cup semi-final), 16 November 2003 (England all-time record)

**Scoring in all ways in a game (try, conversion, penalty goal and a drop goal):** ENGLAND v Wales at Twickenham (Six Nations Championship), 23 March 2002 and ENGLAND v New Zealand at Twickenham, 9 November 2002

# My fantasy XV

**Inga Tuigamala**

**Frank Bunce**

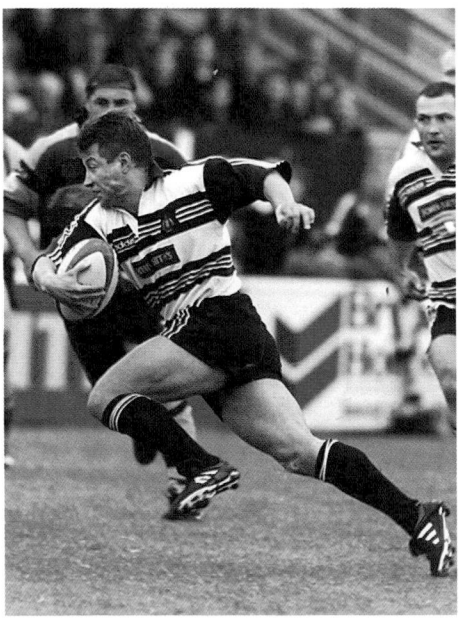

**Rob Andrew**

**Gary Armstrong**

**Jonathan Davies**

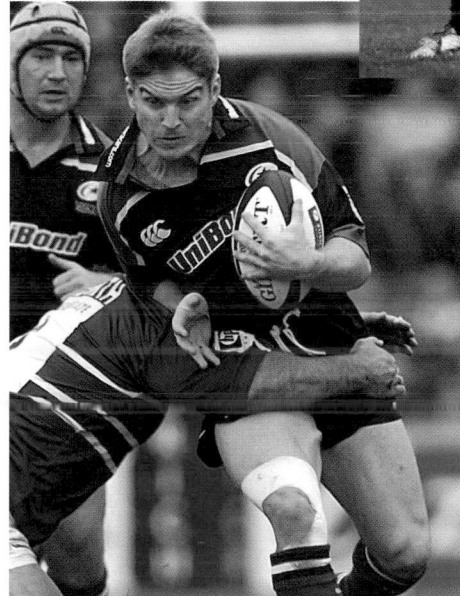

**Tim Horan**

## BACKS

### Full back: JONATHAN DAVIES

A controversial choice perhaps but Davies was so far ahead of his time in line running, side stepping and speed. He was devastating and would be the first point of attack in my side.

### Right wing: INGA TUIGAMALA

Tuigamala was one of the most gifted individuals I have played with not least because of his great size and power. He had some of the best footwork in the game and always seemed to have a smile on his face.

### Outside centre: FRANK BUNCE

Bunce was a very honest hard-working player with all the skills. Above all he had incredible defensive technique and aggression, the type of unsung hero every side needs.

### Inside centre: TIM HORAN

I have selected Horan for his sheer consistency and level of world-class performances. That did not change when he came over to England to play for Saracens and was the star of the 1999 World Cup, overcoming a career-threatening knee injury.

### Left wing: JASON ROBINSON

Robinson broke the mould. One of the most impressive players there has been for the ability to beat opponents and the quality of his footwork. When I first saw him, I couldn't believe what he could do. He made a huge impression on me.

**Jason Robinson**

### Fly half: ROB ANDREW

Andrew's ability to control a game and his understanding of the game were second to none. He has had a huge effect on my career. People do not always appreciate what it takes to win, and Rob was a winner.

### Scrum half: GARY ARMSTRONG

He took on so much responsibility with such humility and helped me in the early stages of my career. We called him the 'junk yard dog' as I've never seen anyone so tough.

HOW TO PLAY RUGBY MY WAY

# FORWARDS

### Loosehead prop: JASON LEONARD

Leonard's durability and his ability to play at the very top for so long was astonishing. He has such a wonderful personality. The way he came back from a serious neck injury without missing a game for England shows what is possible.

### Hooker: SEAN FITZPATRICK

The hard man of the New Zealand front row for so long with tremendous leadership qualities. He was the most fierce of competitors who knew what it took to win and was the most capped forward in the world until Leonard passed him.

### Tighthead prop: PIETER DE VILLIERS

The Springbok-born Frenchman from Stade Français has great pace and mobility with the ball for a prop and can also physically dominate his opponent.

### Second row: MARTIN JOHNSON

Need I say more?

### Second row: IAN JONES

A supreme operator at the line out, with his superb technique and athleticism. He may have been a string bean but few if any got the better of him.

### Blindside flanker: MICHAEL JONES

For his sheer impact. He was one of my brother's and my favourites. The 'Ice-man' as he was known was way ahead of his time. He was so humble and such a man of principle that he refused to play on a Sunday. He also re-invented himself at number 6 after a serious knee injury.

### Openside flanker: RICHARD HILL and NEIL BACK

I can't split them. Two players I have had the pleasure of playing with for a long time who made life a lot easier for me than it probably should have been.

### Number 8: PAT LAM

Lammy is as good a reader of the game as there has ever been. Born with rugby in his blood he is always incredible to watch.

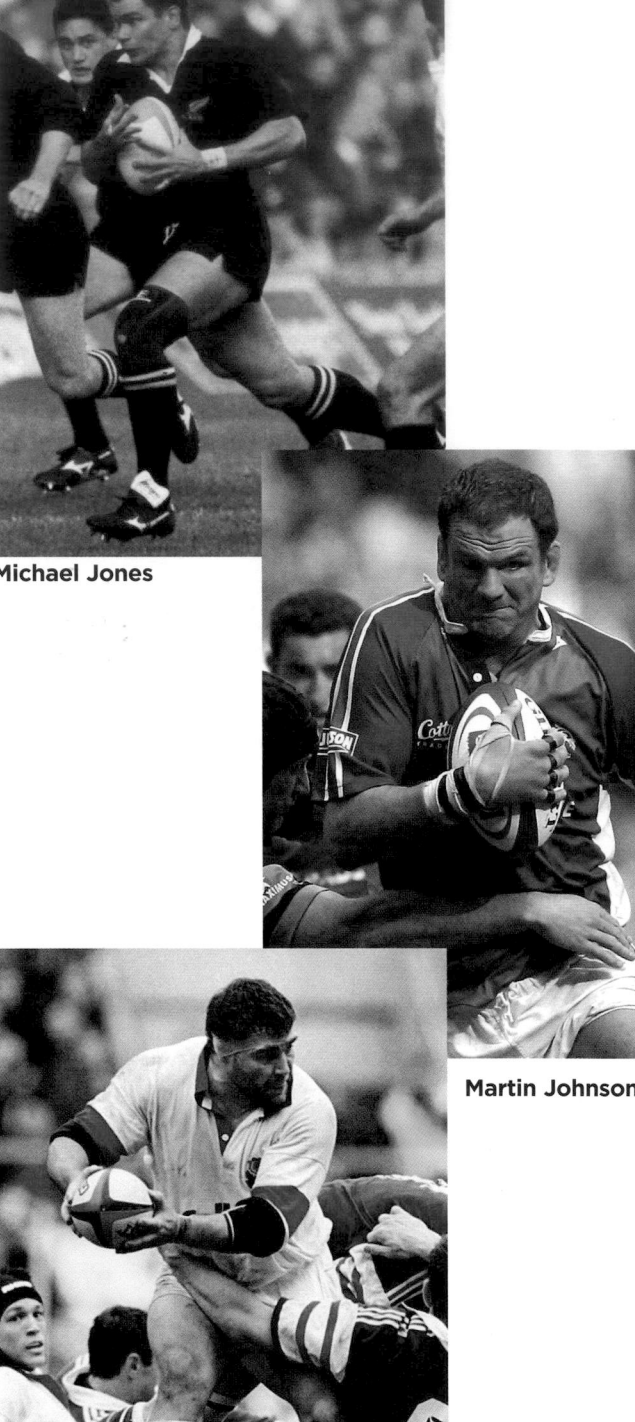

Michael Jones

Martin Johnson

Jason Leonard

Richard Hill

Pat Lam

Neil Back

Ian Jones

Sean Fitzpatrick

Pieter de Villiers

HOW TO PLAY RUGBY MY WAY

# Picture credits

All pictures copyright of Getty Images/Gary Prior except those listed below.
Diagrams supplied by Hardlines.